Father, I Love You

Joyce E Chapman With Terry Ruhl
and Jennifer Wendell

AuthorHouse™
1663 Liberty Drive
Bloomington, IN 47403
www.authorhouse.com
Phone: 1-800-839-8640

© 2009 Joyce E Chapman With Terry Ruhl and Jennifer Wendell. All rights reserved.

No part of this book may be reproduced, stored in a retrieval system, or transmitted by any means without the written permission of the author.

First published by AuthorHouse 12/22/2009

ISBN: 978-1-4490-4419-0 (e)
ISBN: 978-1-4490-4417-6 (sc)
ISBN: 978-1-4490-4418-3 (hc)

Library of Congress Control Number: 2009912728

Printed in the United States of America
Bloomington, Indiana

This book is printed on acid-free paper.

With joy unspeakable
Joyce E. Chapman
♡ Phil 4:6-8

DEDICATION

To my mom, Elaine Cole,
who gave me everything I needed
to start life's journey, including
Christ in my life,
and
to my husband, Bill,
who travels with me and gives me
everything I need for the stay.

ACKNOWLEDGEMENTS

Nothing out of our realm of normal activities is accomplished without inspiration, dedication, perspiration (figuratively speaking), agitation (in small degrees), and collaboration. I thank You, heavenly Father, for the inspiration.

Thank you Terry and Jennifer for the hours of collaboration you spent on finalizing these letters. Thank you my wonderful family, friends, strangers, and church family, alike, who have provided human creativity, inspiration and encouragement to undertake and to continue through to the completion of these letters. Thank you to my sister, Faith Bennett for the mini thoughts following the titles. I love them.

Table of Contents

Introduction	xiii
Caught Up in the Holiday Web	1
One Foot in Front of the Other	3
Satisfaction Guaranteed	5
The Sweet, the Salty, and the Spicy-Sweet	7
Now I Lay Me Down to Sleep (?)	9
What a Family	11
I've Got Mail	13
A Bad Hair Day	15
Praise the Lord (And Pass the Blessings)	17
One Building Block at a Time	19
Lost in a Maze of Corn	21
Welcome! Come on In!	23
The Whole Story	25
Winds of Confusion	27
The Power of Rejoicing	29
Send the Light	31
The Doctor Will See You Now #1—Where Can I Go?	34
The Doctor Will See You Now #2—He's My Doctor? He Takes Good Care of Me!	36
Wheelchairs and Wisdom #1 From Growing Pains to Physical Pain	38
Wheelchairs and Wisdom #2 Pain Relief	40
What I Love About My Church	42
Coffee Time	44
Burdens and Expectations	46
Free for the Asking	48
Happy Anniversary	50
A Beautiful Bouquet of Flowers	52
When I Become Old(er)	54
Problems, Potholes, and Praise	56
Buds, Blossoms, and Fruit	58
Umbrellas 101	60
More than the Average Sign	62
Lost in the Empty Well	66

Hair Today, But Gone Tomorrow	68
Hand in the Cookie Jar	71
Look Out for that Door	73
Gather Me Up, Father #1 The Dawning	75
Gather Me Up, Father #2 Front Row Viewing	76
Adopt-A-Highway	78
Old Dogs and New Lessons	80
Bystander or Participant	82
Wings of Iron Over a Sea of Glass	84
A Mountain Railroad	87
A Faithful Sower of Seed	89
Faith, Praise, and Faithfulness	92
Friends, Friendship, and Fraternity	95
Little Is Much	98
As Soft As a Lamb's Ear	100
Come and Dine	102
The Real Deal	104
A View from the Top	106
Life Is Like a Peanut Butter Cracker	108
What's Under the Cover?	110
There's a Rocky Road Ahead—Maybe.	112
Let the Son Shine In—and Out	114
A Second Look at Light, Fluffy Clouds	117
Mirror, Mirror on the Wall	119
Second-Hand Blessings	121
Showers of Blessings	123
Pillows of Clouds	125
It's What's Underneath that Counts	126
When Is a Leaf Not a Leaf	128
Can You Hear Me Now?	130
To Hesitate or Not to Hesitate	132
Take Your Medicine for a Walk Day	134
Green, Green Grass of Home	136
Ouch! The Yo-Yo Syndrome	139
Into Each Life	141
I See You	143
Bloom Where You're Planted	145

Olympic "Champions"	148
Everyday Is a Payday	151
Broken Fences	154
An Amazing Blanket of White	156
The Good News	158
Freedom Isn't Free	160

INTRODUCTION

Christ spoke to us many times in Scripture through the use of parables. He taught us by using things familiar to us: things we see and/or use daily. We can follow His example and use it to inspire us at any time and under any circumstances. We simply need to "think beyond the confines of the box."

As children, we were able to see beyond the object itself and find some wonderful meaning: a cloud could be a ship sailing across the sky; a fish could be a submarine leading to all kinds of adventures—it was called a "healthy imagination."

As adults, we have the ability to discipline that imagination and use it for inspiration to glory in our salvation, praise our Lord, find the joy of the Spirit, or simply learn a valuable lesson in answer to prayer. When life's road gets "bumpy," we have the ability to stop. To look for inspiration, "Stop," is the defining word. We can look to prayer, Scripture, or look beyond the "confines of the box" to give the Spirit a door through which He directs, instructs, or convicts as needed. It is our job to search, focus, and "listen" for the answer. This book is a reflection of how looking beyond the confines of the box is a tool that can be used for adoration, praise, and inspiration.

But how do we look beyond the box? Knowing Scripture and the Bible as much as individually possible is a great start. We are told in II Timothy 3:16 that, *All scripture is given by inspiration of God, and is profitable for doctrine, for reproof, for reflection, for instruction in righteousness.* This, praise God, is an ongoing blessing. He does not expect us to know everything at once. We can serve with what we do know and continue to grow in His Word and in obedience from this point forward. The more we know, however, the more inspiration He will give to us.

We start from what we know in life and convert that into higher thoughts of righteousness, love, or praise. We forget the "obvious" and look beyond the focal point. To see the "real" thing, we need to look much deeper. We need to "consider" whatever the subject is in light of God's creation. Christ gave us a perfect example:

> *"**Consider** the lilies of the field, how they grow; they toil not, neither do they spin: And yet I say unto you, That even Solomon in all his glory was not arrayed like one of these."* --Matthew 6: 28-29. (emphasis mine)

In describing the lilies, Christ looks beyond their obvious qualities. He doesn't describe how beautiful they are. He doesn't even mention the obvious. Instead, He notices the deeper aspects of the flowers.

We all, at times, need inspiration to help us get through the day and to keep our minds on the right track for living a Christian life. It is so easy to get caught up in the busyness and emotion of this world. Christ, however, cautioned us not to do so, but instead to consider the miracles around us, to be in awe of God's creation and to learn.

These letters, from the author's heart, are letters of praise, petition, and question to the heavenly Father, drawn upon the author's consideration of His creation and framed in His Word, as set forth in the King James Bible. It is the prayer of the author that these pages show the reader examples of a different way to look at what is observed or experienced on a daily basis. When inspiration is needed, we can contemplate fully what is seen or experienced and turn that into food for thought. By physically searching Scripture or recalling what we have learned from Scripture, we can convert what we "see" into what we feel and have been inspired to feel, leading to inspirational and emotional growth.

One final matter of explanation: The author has taken literary license in capitalizing any noun or pronoun referring to

God the Father. This is out of personal respect and is strictly a personal choice.

> Psalm 19:14 says it so well for us: *"Let the words of my mouth, and the meditations of my heart, be acceptable in thy sight, O Lord, my strength and my redeemer."*

CAUGHT UP IN THE HOLIDAY WEB

*Look where you're going.
A careless stroll through life could trip you up.*

Oh, Father, we don't want to admit it or even think it, but what pitiful, fragile creatures we are. I went shopping today: the stores were crowded, the traffic was terrible, and people were rude—pushing, shoving, scowling, rushing, and everything **but** the Christmas spirit. I came home in a terrible mood. I was caught up in a holiday web spun by a "spider" with legs made up of stress, hustle and bustle, lack of direction, unnecessary extravagance, expectations, no expectations, obligation vs. love, and guilt. Why did I let myself become so entangled?

I must have done many things that didn't glorify You, Father. For this, I am truly sorry; that is why I am here, now. I don't like being this way. I need to stop and spend some time with You to put the pieces of my spirit back together **and** in the right order. Please let me focus on the meaning of the "holiday," Father.

Upon reflection, my first mistake was getting lost in holiday shopping instead of enjoying Christmas preparations. Christmas is a time to reflect on Your goodness and greatness. You are a good God. You are a great God. You are a faithful God.

What should occupy my mind during this season? You? Your Word? family? friends? the less fortunate? strangers? my church? "Yes" to all of these, Father. My mind should be filled with love and thoughts of all of these, but in particular You and Jesus Christ. You tell me in Philippians 4:8 *"Finally, brethren, whatsoever things are true, whatsoever things are honest, whatsoever things are just, whatsoever things are pure, whatsoever things are lovely, whatsoever things are of good report: if there be any virtue and if there be any praise, think on these things."*

Your Word came as flesh to dwell among us in the person of Jesus Christ. It is Christmas first, not just a holiday—Christmas, the birth of Your Son, my Savior. What a glorious occasion: not just the beginning of a child's life, but the beginning of a new life for *all* of Your children. It was the beginning of our education; it was the beginning of a clean slate; it was the beginning of our path to eternity with You.

Lord, please grant me the grace to slow down, dwell on the important things, and live the Christian example of the Christmas season. Thank You for Your gift, Your promise, and Your future plans for me.

I love You.

ONE FOOT IN FRONT OF THE OTHER

How do you eat an elephant?
You have to eat it one bite at a time.

I went for my walk today, Father. I was tired and didn't want to do it. You've heard it before, Father, "Do I have to?" with a little whine thrown in. I kept thinking, "one foot in front of the other; one foot in front of the other"—and I did finish my walk. All it took was placing one foot in front of the other—again and again—not necessarily thinking about the step itself, but thinking about the importance of finishing the task. And, it did feel so good when the task was finished.

I was reminded of Your Word: *"Wherefore seeing we also are compassed about with so great a cloud of witnesses, let us lay aside every weight, and the sin which doth so easily beset us, and let us run with patience the race that is set before us, Looking unto Jesus the author and finisher of our faith; who for the joy that was set before him endured the cross, despising the shame, and is set down at the right hand of the Throne of God."* --Hebrews 12: 1-2

Endurance, Father--Christ didn't quit or give up. He had a task to do and He completed that task. Christ paid it all out of love. I know from Scripture that He didn't want to die. I know He asked for the task before Him to be removed—if it was Your will. That's the key, Father—Your will.

I'm human, and as such, I am a creature of the flesh. "I don't feel like doing it," or worse yet, in some cases, "I feel like doing it" seems to cross my mind multiple times a day. I need to run the race to righteousness—one step at a time. I will finish the race, won't I, Father—one step at a time? If I stumble, as I often do, You will catch me and pick me up if I reach out to You.

I must run with patience, joy, might, and persistence. I must enlist what I have been taught, and stretch myself more and more each day.

I am told: *"Whatsoever thy hand findeth to do, do it with thy might; for there is no work, nor device, nor knowledge, nor wisdom, in the grave, whither thou goest."* --Ecclesiastes 9:10

Thank You for a track on which to run and for Christ who taught me how to run the race. Thank You for Your Word which sets forth the straight and narrow path leading me to the finish line.

I love You.

SATISFACTION GUARANTEED

A grateful heart has the blessings of the Spirit.

Father, when I started our car this morning, I was greeted by a quiet, smooth-running engine. I have never paid particular attention to this blessing. Thoughts started knocking at my heart's door: a message is trying to get through to me. Why is it that when things are going along smoothly, I accept them without thought other than, "That's the way it is supposed to "run." I may just continue with what I'm doing without any thought towards the blessing that I'm receiving.

I would never overlook my gratitude toward someone's kind and thoughtful action. I would thank them and show my appreciation in an appropriate way. But, when it is a life's blessing coming from You, I am slow to recognize the magnitude of Your goodness or to realize that it is, indeed, a blessing. I am reminded in I Thessalonians 5:18: *"In every thing give thanks: for this is the will of God in Christ Jesus concerning you."*

Mom has a bookmark which has the following thoughts: "Father, help me commit each day to You. Help me keep You uppermost in my thoughts and grant me the grace to let Your love shine in my eyes and for Your praise ever continue to leave my lips." The bookmark was from Dr. Charles Stanley and the In Touch Ministries. It spoke to me. Thank You, Father, for the author of these thoughts and the application they brought to my heart. The quote above and the following quotes are theirs, Father, but the lessons learned are mine.

I considered the above thoughts in connection with unrecognized blessings and appropriate gratitude.

A simple "thank You for awakening to a new morning" would be appropriate. "A prayer to start the day with rejoicing and praise" would be appropriate; "keeping You on my heart and lips throughout the day" would be appropriate; "a praise for Your promise in Lamentations 3: 22-23 that Your loving kindness never ceases" would be appropriate; and a "praise that Your compassion never fails, but is new every morning," would be appropriate.

Oh, Father, how often I take these gifts for granted. Thank You for reminding me of these things that I have to be thankful for. Thank You, also, Father, for a husband who keeps the car maintained and safe for me. Bill is, indeed, Your greatest earthly gift to me. Help me, Father, to be the wife he needs.

I thank You, Father, for all of Your blessings, seen and unseen. From You they are boundless and custom-made. And, from You, they come with the Creator's guarantee of satisfaction.

I love You.

THE SWEET, THE SALTY, AND THE SPICY-SWEET

*A tool box holds a tool for every job.
You just need to pick out the right one—choose wisely.*

Father, today I prepared a graduation present for my friend. She is graduating from Bible College.

The gift I have prepared is very simple: a bowl divided into three equal sections, each section containing a different flavor of party mix. If she feels the need for something sweet, she can choose that; if she wants something salty, she chooses another flavor; and, if she wants something spicy-sweet, the third would be her choice. She has a gift from which she can choose according to her need—the same gift, but freedom to choose according to her individual need at the time—any time.

I am reminded of You, Father. You also have given me three distinct "flavors" of Your divinity: the Father, the Son, and the Holy Spirit, each division with its own texture and satisfaction, depending on my individual need at the time.

When I need the sweet, I can look to Your sweet Holy Spirit. I can look to the Holy Spirit for Your guidance, inspiration, and, yes, even correction or chastisement, speaking directly to me from You.

When I need to make sure my witnessing is not losing its savor, I can reach out for You, Father, for, like salt, without savor, it is ineffective. I am told this in Luke 14:34: *"Salt is good: but if the salt have lost his savour, wherewith shall it be seasoned?"*

When I need to express my gratitude and praise for my eternal Salvation, I look to Your Son, Jesus Christ, who gave His sweet life so my life will have more flavor.

When I am in the need of pouring out love, praise, and glory for all that is around me and my heart will not hold another ounce of Your goodness without feeling as though it will explode, I seek to give You praise. Without You, life is without flavor because the Father, the Son, and the Holy Spirit are the spices of my life.

Thank You, Father, for all of these.

I love You.

NOW I LAY ME DOWN TO SLEEP (?)

*Even if you didn't have a good home life,
you have the power to give it.*

Yesterday was Dad's birthday. You know him, Father. He's Your son, Joe, and is with You now. He has been gone from us for years, but it is still hard to think about him without experiencing a flood of memories. I was so emotionally charged: some sad, some glad, but all with gratitude and praise for Your gift of my family. Because of these memories, I slept very little last night.

I spent most of the night thinking about my family: Dad's influence in my life, Mom's influence, and things and times the family shared during my growing-up years. I was truly blessed. As You promised in Proverbs 20:7, *"The just man walketh in his integrity: his children are blessed after him."*

I remembered the family times we had. I remembered the singing and gospel "jam" sessions around the piano. I treasured, again, the times Dad read "the classics" to us and Mom shared Your Word with us—and the sacrifices Mom and Dad made to make our home warm and comfortable. I thought, a day of play is soon forgotten, but simple moments of true family togetherness is with us always. Another blessing!

Your Word instructs us about the importance of training a child in Godly paths. I thought of the things Dad taught us: work ethics, love of nature, conservation of our environment—anything he taught his Boy Scouts he tried to teach his girls.

I also thought of the things Mom taught us by example: creating a comfortable, clean home, her consistent church attendance, her teaching in the Sunday school, her working in the church kitchen and cleaning the church, her singing in the choir, and her willingness to do anything else that needed to be done. I am so thankful that my parents followed the Biblical way as instructed in Proverbs 22:6, *"Train up a child in the way he should go: and when he is old, he will not depart from it."*

I began to wonder, Father, am I doing enough? What am I doing, Father? Am I physically capable of doing more? Of course, I am! What? I don't know, but I do know that You will let me know when it's time to put in more time and effort to mentor someone, time to encourage, or time to rest. I want to be available for Your call. Am I willing to listen to the prompting of Your Spirit? I pray, Father, I prove willing. Help me to ask for guidance and listen for the Spirit's promptings.

Thank You so much, Father, for giving me a Christian heritage with a Godly, loving, and caring upbringing filled with music and a love of nature. I know I was, and am, truly blessed. Of one thing, I am certain: When I can't sleep, it is generally because I have things to ponder. These things produce inspiration, enlightenment, and memories, which bring about gratitude to the Maker of all things good. Thank You, Father, for memories that create renewal and wake up my slumbering praise.

I love You.

WHAT A FAMILY

Sisters and friends stick together; they don't stick each other.

What a trip, Father. I was in Los Angeles with my extended family this weekend. They are wonderful. Thank You for each of them, and please bless them. I love them all so very much.

It was good to see my "sisters" again. Each of us has a distinct personality. I guess if we were all the same, some of us would be unnecessary. Praise You, Father, that that isn't true.

You have given each of us a purpose, but each of us has some rough spots. Similarly, You have given every rose its thorns, yet the thorns are a planned part of the rose. If we want to glory in the beauty of the rose, we learn to avoid the thorns (not approve of them, but accept them) and thereby admire Your workmanship.

Some of ***our*** "thorns" are external; others are, figuratively speaking, internal. They are not flaws; they, like real thorns, are a part of the creation. Our external thorns, Father, those in the open, are obvious and can be avoided with caution. It's the internal thorns attached to the rose in each of us, however, which may cause the real damage. They can directly pierce the heart and grieve the Spirit. These thorns we ***must*** turn over to You for removal.

Your Son, Jesus Christ, wore a crown of thorns for me. He took personal responsibility for my internal thorns, and I need only ask Him to remove some of these hurtful extensions of my personality.

Christ is the example of true love, which demands forgiveness and gives us the ability to look beyond the thorns to see only the beauty. In Ephesians 4:32 You remind me of Christ's "type" of love: *"And be ye kind one to another, tenderhearted, forgiving one another, even as God for Christ's sake hath forgiven you."*

As Your children, we can choose to follow Christ's example. If we do, we will be able to see Your beauty all around us. If we do not, the "thorns" will keep us from the wonders that You make available to us.

You have given me a loving extended family. I pray they will forgive my rough spots, thorns and all, accept my shortcomings, and look for the beauty deep inside. I pray they will see You in my example, and overlook the thorns I have collected along the way.

I love You.

I'VE GOT MAIL

*What few little seeds we pass to others may be
the only seeds they have to plant.*

Today I got a message from a friend, Father, and it came in the form of an e-mail. E-mail can be a good or a bad thing. It is the same as other things in my earthly existence: it depends on how I use it or respond to it.

When an e-mail is good, I put it into printed form and look at it now and again. I cherish it, think about it, and respond to it, if necessary. If it is undesirable (or "bad"), I delete it, forget about it, and just leave it at that. I don't immediately delete the good things, and I don't even open the "bad" things.

At times e-mail requires follow-up action. If something is particularly good, I forward it to someone I care about or to someone who expresses a need for the message. I forward to others only that which is good to share—that which is inspiring, informative, delightful, helpful, and/or just plain good food for thought.

The Bible says that the rain falls on the just and the unjust. Bad things sometimes happen to good people. It is when bad things may happen that I am reminded that You, Father, have sent me a message in the Bible—Eternity Mail. Your Word is already printed out. I can pull it out and look at it at any time. It is always filled with a "good" message: inspiring, informative, delightful, helpful, and full of food for thought. Like a good e-mail, Your Word is designed to be shared; it is too good not to. Not a day goes by that I can't pull something from Your Word for solution to problems or the strength to get through another trial. I do need to open it to do that, however. If I do as I should, I will not only read the Word but do what I am told to do. You told us in Your Word: *"But he said, Yea rather, blessed are they that hear the word of God, **and** keep it."* --Luke 11:28. (emphasis mine)

I don't personally know what it was like in the time of Christ, Father, but You have told me in Your Word. I do know what my future will be, Father, because You have told me in Your Word. And, Father, I know what the future of those who do not know You or accept You will be, because You have also told me that in Your Word.

Oh, Father, please grant me the grace to share Your Word and Your presence with those who do not know You or are unsure of where they will spend eternity, for their eternity is a devastating story. Your story, however, is simple: it is a simple matter to accept Your gift. It is a simple process, but it came at a very high cost to You and Christ.

Thank You, Father, for Your daily Eternity Mail. It is always welcome, refreshing, and can be shared endlessly with others. I look forward to tomorrow's message.

I love You.

A BAD HAIR DAY

A bad hair day is only bad until you do something about it.

I was sitting in a waiting room today, Father. There were three friendly ladies sitting there just waiting to be seen—so I saw them. Two of the ladies were wearing cute little hats and I complimented them on how "snazzy" they looked. They smiled, and we started visiting back and forth. It was a really nice way to wait. In fact, waiting in this instance was a blessing.

During the course of our conversation, one of the ladies told me she had made the hats they were wearing, and she sells the hats at craft fairs. She calls them "Bad-Hair-Day Hats." "What a great idea," I thought—but, I also knew there was a lesson in there somewhere for me, so I've been pondering her comment, Father—and it has been a real joy.

As a human, I have "bad hair days." These are days when things (and/or people) just don't seem to cooperate with me; I feel less than I could or should be; I don't want anyone to see me—or worse than that, I don't want to see or be around anyone. If it were actually a bad hair problem, I would know what to do—I would go to my hair dresser and let her make it right.

But life isn't that simple when I'm the one "all messed up," is it Father? Or maybe it is that simple. You and Jesus Christ make everything all right. Like the wonderful song by Cleavant Derricks says, "A Little Talk with Jesus Makes It Right." All I need to do is tell Him my cares and sorrows. My cares and sorrows always seem like such heavy burdens, but in reality they are small in comparison to many other people's problems. I just need someone to help me carry my burden and to know that someone does care about what I am going through.

I further pondered my "bad hair days" and considered that You and Christ are my "bad-hair-day hats"—meaning it as a loving, respectful illustration. If I am having a bad hair day from an unknown source, I choose to look to Your creation and its beauty, to ponder Your promises, to feel Your goodness, or to ask You for Your mercy and grace.

Christ can cover my unsightliness when I need forgiveness for my transgressions and am feeling pretty "soiled" and unmanageable. When I go to You through Him and ask for forgiveness, I am covered with His love and grace; He washes away the dirt—and everything is made all right by His grace and love. When He's finished, it feels *so* good!

My bad hair day should not be exposed to the masses, but at times there isn't much I feel I can do about it on my own. With You, however, that is a different story because as Your word tells me in Matthew 19:26, all things are possible with You.

Thank You, Father, for my family and for my church family. They may see me on a bad hair day but still love me and see my potential. Thank You for Your unfailing love, for covering me with Your blessings, and for giving this child the JOY of the Spirit. With that JOY, I can keep my "bad hair days" under my "hat" so they aren't displayed to others I meet. I want to be groomed and covered by You so others will see only Your excellence.

I love You.

PRAISE THE LORD
(And Pass the Blessings)

When you add love, blessings grow.

Bill woke me up this morning with our usual smooch, Father. It's a small thing, but I must admit it is a great way to wake up.

One of my daily blessings is Bill's preparation of the morning coffee before he leaves for his walk. His coffee is the best! The aroma hits first. The anticipation starts to fill every part of my being. My nose breathes in the aroma; my mind is filled with thoughts of spending time with my family.

After preparing the coffee this morning, Bill went for his walk in our beautiful city park. Mom was still asleep, so I came to You for our quiet time together. It is such an important time of day. This morning, Father, as usual, a lot was taken off of my mind just from spending time with You. I gained peace and started my day out right. Thank You.

When I complete my quiet time with You, my heart was still full. My conviction is that You, Father, are on Your throne, and *all* is well. I look forward to Bill's returning from his walk and to Mom's waking up and getting her cat, Max, fed and "loved up." I so look forward to my morning time with Bill, Mom, and Max.

Our family time generally takes place on the back patio where we drink in the beauty of Your beautiful flowers and sip our coffee. Mom and I talk about the flowers and the yard, and Bill does his best to look and act interested. Or he just spends time with us in Your great outside. And, oh, yes, Max surveys his kingdom with great anticipation of seeing and playing with one of Your "critters." Thank You, Father, for the ones I live with and love—and for our mornings together.

Once finished with our time together and ready to start our individual days, the coffee time has turned out to be everything we had anticipated and had hoped for. We ultimately received great satisfaction from taking the time to visit and just be together.

My time with my family reminds me of my time with You, Father. I go into my quiet room to be with You, undisturbed and uninhibited, surrounded by my thoughts, expectations, praise, and petitions. I approach You in great anticipation of my heart being filled with joy, my burdens being lightened, and my prayers being answered. You, Father, ask only for my love, praise, and faithfulness.

I again anticipate—I anticipate Your love, mercy, forgiveness, and grace. You, Father, ask only for my obedience, gratitude, and steadfastness in following Christ's example.

We share. I can talk with You about things other people would not be interested in—or that I feel would be an unfair burden for them. I don't need to worry about coming up with interesting things to talk about with You because interest is not a consideration as long as I am sincere. I don't have to be self-conscious about showing emotion or about stumbling over my words because it isn't the mouth that is important: it's the heart, not the words, that is heard. You know the words I stumble over, and Your answers to my prayers assure me time and time again that You heard and understood my heart. This time with You is the most precious part of my day, Father. You are an awesome God. *"To the end that my glory may sing praise to thee, and not be silent. O LORD my God, I will give thanks unto thee for ever."* --Psalm 30:12

Every time I praise You and petition You, You pass the blessings to me. Thank You for being so faithful to Your weak child. Thank You for being there, always, for our visit. Thank You for Your everlasting mercies and grace. Father, I thank You for the right to praise You as my heavenly Father—and please grant me the grace to pass Your blessings on to others.

I love You.

ONE BUILDING BLOCK AT A TIME

Block by block makes a structure. Careless dumping makes a heap.

Father, I was watching a couple of children build a house out of building blocks. I thought about that building block creation and realized that the foundation was the most important part of the structure: it was the key to a stable, finished house.

The children's house was built one block at a time. Each block was carefully stacked on top of another block, on top of another block, and on and on it goes—all starting from a set, firm foundation. If the foundation was not properly set, the blocks tumbled down.

If a block was placed out of order, the entire structure was skewed. If, however, each block was placed carefully, the building was strengthened for the next level. If a block was found to be out of place, the children went back and reset that block and then they were back on the right path.

The children kept adding block upon block upon block, and it became easier to see the design that they had in mind. It also became easier to see what needed to be changed. It wasn't perfect; maybe not what the children originally had in mind, but when all of the blocks had been added with thought, it was a house—and, there was no need to start over from scratch. It was a very forgiving project.

My Christian life is a lot like that, isn't it, Father? I have a solid foundation in the saving knowledge and acceptance of Jesus Christ. I have Your plan, My Creator's plan, to follow, and I can and should refer to this plan, Your Word, every step of the way. I can start building My Christian life, precept upon Biblical precept, as soon as the foundation is set.

My Christian life is something like a spiral of experience. Each turn of the spiral prepares me for the next experience (much like one level of blocks prepared the children for the next level of blocks). If I get a precept out of order or overlook it, I will be unprepared for the next turn of the spiral. But if a precept is out of order, once corrected, I am prepared for the next challenge. Again, it is a very "forgiving" endeavor.

And so I asked myself, "Is my life built on a solid foundation?" Your Word tells me in Matthew 7:24-27: *"Therefore whosoever heareth these sayings of mine, and doeth them, I will liken him unto a wise man, which built his house upon a rock: And the rain descended, and the floods came, and the winds blew, and beat upon that house; and it fell not: for it was founded upon a rock. And every one that heareth these sayings of mine, and doeth them not, shall be likened unto a foolish man, which built his house upon the sand: And the rain descended, and the floods came, and the winds blew, and beat upon that house; and it fell: and great was the fall of it."* Thanks to You, Father, and Jesus Christ my rock, my foundation, and my salvation, I am.

Do I build my life precept by Biblical precept, or do I go through each day without following the blueprint You so lovingly have drawn out for me? I try, Father, but I have many of Your precepts out of order. I need to do some correcting. Thank You, Father, for Your Word as it tells me how to get them back in order.

Is my house in order? We're working on it, aren't we, Father? Which precepts need to be straightened out? If I stay in Your Word, You will show me and the Holy Spirit will prompt me according to Your Will. Am I willing to make the corrections as needed? I pray, Father, that I am. I have faith that You will guide me all of the way.

Oh, Father, please grant me the grace to continue considering these questions in depth in my quiet time with You.

I look forward to claiming the promise that if I build precept upon Biblical precept, my life, when finished, will be complete, strong, beautiful, and worth the work. Praise You, Father, for giving me Your Son, Jesus Christ as my foundation.

I love You.

LOST IN A MAZE OF CORN

*God may not cause life's maze,
but He is an amazing guide through it.*

Father, it is so good to share special things about my day with You. Today Bill and I went with our son and two of our grandchildren to a corn maze. The "kids" live in Idaho, as You know, so a corn maze is quite easy to find—it might take a few miles, but there is always one available. As Grandpa, Dad, and kids proceeded to go through the maze, I sat in the car and pondered the wonders of a maze and the fun that they were going to have.

I thought about the false starts, the wrong turns, the misleading walls, and all of the blocks in the path of reaching the goal. I thought about the interim goal in this maze: **finding the bridge**.

I then thought about the feeling of helplessness that accompanies being lost, even if it is for only a few minutes—but then, they did have Dad and Grandpa to help them get back on track.

In considering the maze and the fun we were having (Yes, me too; I was having fun thinking about You.), I thought about my staying in the car. I thought, laughing at myself, that the type of maze I would enjoy would be one with a straight line from the entry to the exit.

What about my life? My life is a maze from beginning to the end. I have choices facing me every step of the way. Do I turn left? right? go straight? What do I do? I cry from within; "Someone, please help me and show me the way!" Father!

Father, You **did not** put the blocks, turns, and twists in the way of life's journey. You did, however, put a bridge in there. You gave me Your Son, Jesus Christ, as the bridge from death to life. *"Jesus saith unto him, I am the way, the truth, and the life: no man cometh unto the Father, but by me."* --John 14:6

From the point of salvation, You gave me a straight line to travel to the end of my time on earth.

You told me in Your Word how to find the bridge. You gave me a map to follow to find You. If I get lost along the way, all I have to do is to call out to You and You will direct my feet. You *did* tell me that I should not turn to the right or to the left. You told me to walk the straight and narrow path and it would lead me to You.

When I do get a little lost, I tend to get a little emotionally anxious (a kind understatement). When I am in the depth of this *panic*, I get that feeling of overwhelming helplessness. I also may feel a little ridiculous because I didn't follow the path set out for me—and it was laid out so simply and clearly in Your Word.

You *are* always with me, Father, so I will be found. I don't need to worry. I just need to take a minute to talk with You (or, depending on how deeply lost in the maze I am, a longer period of time). I can rely on You. You tell me this in Philippians 4: 6-8. After all, You did build the path and know how to direct me through it. I just need to conform my steps to the directions You have given me. I would continue to be lost in this world if I did not.

Father, even the best of Your children get temporarily lost. Sometimes minds wander from the straight path, hearts may take a few bumps along the way, but souls are protected for eternity from getting lost from You.

Praise You, Father. I am so very thankful for my remarkable God. You are amazing.

I love You.

WELCOME! COME ON IN!

*Don't share the bad stuff.
There's so much good to share.*

I have felt better, Father. This week I've had a virus. It started with one household member and before long it spread throughout the whole household.

During this period of time, we had some thoughtful visitors come to visit us, but we had to tell them there were too many germs inside and they **shouldn't** come and spend time with us. It would be good for us but not for them.

This is such an unpleasant thing to tell a visitor. They came to encourage. They prepared special blessings for the household. They came to pray for the family, and they traveled away from the comfort of their own home to help us. But what else could we do? We didn't want to be responsible for infecting another family and another family and another family. The germs have to stop somewhere.

Sin is a lot like germs, isn't it, Father? It is evil waiting to spread from one person to another person and on and on and on. It takes only the initial exposure and a weakened condition to infect and inflict damage. Sin is all around us; we can't get away from it. If we aren't prepared to combat it, or if we are in a weakened condition, this evil can invade us and take over our otherwise healthy being. There isn't an antibiotic that can cure sin—nothing but You, Your Son, and Your Spirit. It is times like these that we need to invite You to "come on in." You are not in danger of being infected, and You supply cure-alls for the soul.

I was thinking today of some of Your supply of cure-alls that are available to me:

Your Grace is sufficient for all—pure power for my needs.
Your Son's blood gives me a clean slate; an eternity with You and with Him.

Your supremacy gives me courage in this life to meet the battles which I need fight—but not alone anymore.
Your love and faithfulness provide Comfort in times of insecurity.
Your steadfastness and omnipotence yield security and confidence.
Your creation supplies me with opportunities for growth.
Your church family offers fulfillment of life and encouragement in that growth.
Your earthly shepherds feed my spiritual hunger.
Your greatness and unlimited love provide me with a grateful heart and pulls from me all the glory due Your name.
Your Word gives me direction and resolution: past, present and future.
Your promises are available for me to claim, at any time. They are a cure-all for any ill which may come into my life.
Your house, my home church, *is the place for me to be whenever its doors are open.* ***Your home,*** Father, is **the** place for me to dwell for all eternity.

It's all Yours, Father. So many of these things I can only see through my limited human understanding. I'm sure, however, that I have access to everything You have offered, and that I will be welcomed into eternity through Christ's sacrifice on the cross. What a difference it makes: I fail, but I am not defeated. I fall, but You pick up the pieces and put them back together again. I start to stumble, but You keep me grounded. I am feeble, but You are my strength. Thank You, Father, for all of these: To You all glory is given.
  I love You.

THE WHOLE STORY

Big or small, God knows it all.

Just as Exodus thrills my soul and imagination, Philippians feeds my soul and provides the tools necessary to survive in my anxious earthly existence. I am a worrier, Father—but You know that and love me anyway. At times, I know I give You a problem to take care of, but then I don't want to "bother" You so I take it back. Bother **You**: The Supreme Being, the Creator of all things, the Father of all mankind, and the Keeper of Eternity. What am I thinking! My little problems are nothing for You to solve, however, they are a gigantic way in which You show Your continuous love for me. Why do I hold back? Let God be God. To God is the glory! I do, however, know to come to You in *all* things. Of that lesson I am sure.

This is my *"When-I-Don't-Know-What-To-Do"* verse, Father: *"Be careful for nothing; but in every thing by prayer and supplication with thanksgiving, let your requests be made known unto God."* --Philippians 4:6

You tell me what to do when I am feeling anxious, confused, bewildered, and overcome. You don't let me wallow in my helplessness. You give me a way out. You give me a hand up, and You clean up the mess I am in. May I live Your example, Father, and be available and willing to help as an extension of Your love when I have a brother or sister in need.

This, Father, as You know, is my *"Why-Am-I-Doing-This"* verse: *"And the peace of God, which passeth all understanding, shall keep your hearts and minds through Christ Jesus."* --Philippians 4:7

Who could ask for more, Father? What more could I personally ask for than for Your perfect peace in time of stress and confusion.

Your Word further tells me that I don't even have to have an eloquently prepared verbiage. Believe me; I don't have the words when I have my biggest needs. At times the only thing that comes out is "Thank You, Father." This is, however, adequate enough, because as we are told: *"Likewise the Spirit also helpeth our infirmities: for we know not what we should pray for as we ought: but the Spirit itself maketh intercession for us with groanings which cannot be uttered. And he that searcheth the hearts knoweth what is the mind of the Spirit, because he maketh intercession for the saints according to the will of God."* -- Romans 8: 26-27

WOW!

I do so appreciate and cherish these verses in Philippians and the verses in Romans, Father, but I need, at times, to be told step-by-step how to do something.

This verse is my "How-To" verse, Father: *"Finally, brethren, whatsoever things are true, whatsoever things are honest, whatsoever things are just, whatsoever things are pure, whatsoever things are lovely, whatsoever things are of good report; if there be any virtue, and if there be any praise, think on these things."* --Philippians 4: 8

My mind can be filled with many kinds of thoughts: worry, anger, or confusion. I rely on and trust in Your Word, Father. It has not and will not fail me. By following Your Word, I find that in only a few seconds a smile will come across my face and Your peace, Your promised peace which is beyond my earthly understanding, comes and calms my troubled mind. Thank You for Your faithfulness and love.

I love You.

WINDS OF CONFUSION

*When you don't know what to do,
start from the ground (on your knees) up (to God).*

It is just a time of conversation, Father. I do feel so much better after we visit. The winds of confusion in our wonderful country are blowing without mercy. It seem as though things are all out of order: our lives, our families, our cities, our states, our country, our world. What is true? What is not true? What is right? What is not right? Do we go with the winds of change or do we stay with the cleansing, peaceful breeze of what we know is good and what we know is right?

These are rhetorical questions, Father, but I know You know that. As Your children, we know which way the breeze is blowing and how to guard against the damaging winds: You tell us in Your Word. You shelter us in the loving arms of Christ, and You provide help for us in times of devastation. What a joy to cling to during the winds of change.

Pastor was speaking to us this morning (thank You, again, Father, for Pastor and his family) about letting our moderations be known to every man **and woman** (my addition for personal application). *"Let your moderation be known unto all men. The Lord is at hand."* --Philippians 4:5

It is always a right time to let people know, up front, what I am all about: not lip service, but soul service. What am I all about? What do I expect? What will I accept? What will I not accept? These are things people need to know up front. People should not have to guess whether or not I am sincere. If I say it, I must believe it; I must live it; I must show it. If not, shame on me.

I so deeply want the outside to match the inside, Father. It is too easy to feel the right way about something, but not step forward for fear of what someone might think or say. That is just as wrong as stepping forward and saying something, but not believing or living what is coming from my mouth.

Am I easily blown in the wrong direction, Father? Am I all wind and no substance? God forbid! I pray I am steadfast in my belief and in my witnessing. Actions do speak louder than words, and I pray for the grace that my actions and my words work together for Your glory.

Winds are good though, aren't they? They have a purpose: some as warnings, some for benefit, and some are dangerous and come unexpectedly even though they have been building up for a long time.

Your Spirit keeps Your children abreast of the wind conditions. I am cautioned when a wind is turning ugly or dangerous. I am told when a wind is soothing and to enjoy it while it is with me because it will pass. I am warned when a wind is going to be strong, but necessary—prepare for it, this too, shall pass. I am also told by Your Word how to weather a storm. You are my refuge in times of danger. You are my unyielding rock and my salvation. You are all sufficient. You, Father, are the answer to turning the wind of destruction into the gentle breeze. I have no strength without You. But I do need to heed Your warning and follow Your directions for survival.

During our talks, I do feel Your calming my churnings. You have so many examples in Your Word of Your peace. Christ tells me: *"Peace I leave with you, my peace I give unto you: not as the world giveth, give I unto you. Let not your heart be troubled, neither let it be afraid."* --John 14: 27

Even the sea obeys: In Mark 4:39 Christ spoke *". . . Peace, be still."* Peace, be still. With You, now, as in the beginning—You speak; it is executed; it is good. Thank You, Father, for calming the winds of confusion around Your child.

I love You.

THE POWER OF REJOICING

"Rejoice in the Lord always; and again I say, Rejoice."
--Philippians 4:4

You know I love the book of Philippians, Father. It has special meaning to my heart and lingers in my mind. We talked before about my personal limitations—worrying, being **one** of them. I seem to ponder everything "to pieces." There are verses throughout this chapter of Philippians which speak to me in personal application. I understand the principle of the verse, but I ask, on a daily basis, that they speak to me in application, also.

You always give me something. "Rejoice!" This is a picture word, Father. I can visualize the wonderful picture this word unfolds. When a person rejoices, the heart is filled with gratitude and thanksgiving. Cares and everything else of the world seem to fade into the background and/or disappear. A smile replaces a worried frown. Muscles relax, and even, at times, a sigh of relief escapes.

"Relief," another beautiful word, indicates to me that this emotional impact veils life's wrinkles and can make life beautiful, again.

Not all wrinkles are bad, though, Father. Some wrinkles are beautiful—these are wrinkles of experience and weathering storms of life. Other wrinkles are not so beautiful—these are wrinkles of worry, frowning, abuse, and self-inflicted wounds.

I love to think or verbalize throughout the day, "Thank You, Father"—for everything. It puts life into perspective. All good things come from You. Why shouldn't I "Rejoice in the Lord always"?

I must recall, also, that I am to rejoice in all things—the good as well as the bad. I rejoice because it is a part of Your plan or part of Your mercy or a lesson from You. I don't know why bad things happen to good people. I only know that You are there for me—whatever the reason. I do believe in Your miracles, Father.

This leads me to the three other verses in Philippians 4 that I'm pondering today. They are short, but sweet. (Verse 11) *"I can do all things through Christ which strengtheneth me. . . ." (Verses 12-20) "But my God shall supply all your needs according to his riches in glory by Christ Jesus."*

These are powerful verses for Your children, me in particular. Verse 11 reminds me that there are many things I (Your children) consider impossible which are achieved daily with Your intervention. There have been many times when Your hand is obvious to me and I know in my heart that You have answered a particularly difficult situation for me. How? Because, I have thought and thought and searched for a solution to these problems on my own, but nothing comes. Then I pray for Your guidance (which should have been done in the beginning) and before I know it, a solution comes to mind—a solution so unique that I would never, ever have thought of it on my own. The solution is always successful and within my ability to accomplish.

Verse 19 tells me that my needs will not only be supplied, but that the supply is unlimited, because it is in accordance to Your riches in Glory through Christ Jesus. This is pure power, Father, a gift wrapped in a prayer and ours for the asking.

Verse 20 speaks to me as an extension of **"Rejoice in the Lord always."** I do give You glory forever and ever. To the Creator of all things, to the Healer of all wounds, to the Author of eternity, I rejoice always.

I love You.

SEND THE LIGHT

Light must be connected to a power source.
God is the source: plug in and turn on.

It is such a delight to view, to walk in, to sit by, and to drink in the beauty of Your oceans, Father. The first thing I do when I get to visit Your creation is to drink in the beauty. I notice how the beach gently yields to the superiority of the billowing waves, yet it endures the pressure placed on it. The beach is not damaged; it just changes as it is directed by the power of the water. The sand to the water, the water to the sand, intermingled into a beautiful sight: constantly changing, constantly interacting.

This reminds me of Your omnipotence, Father. I must yield to Your power. I will not be damaged; however, I will be changed and conform to Your direction. It is a natural thing for Your child to be continually interacting with You, waiting for the change of tides and moving in accordance with Your directing.

The next thing I do, Father, is to walk the beach—barefooted if possible: the sand is so cool and refreshing. It is soft and gentle to the touch, and clings to the pressures of my footsteps, not leaving unless I "brush" it off. Your Word is much like this to me, Father: refreshing, soft, gentle, but many times has a sharp object which pierces and clings to my heart—it hurts at times because it is convicting, but, unlike the sand, in this case, I dare not become foolish and "brush it off."

While walking on the beach, I notice the breeze. It isn't "freezing." It is cold and this chill makes me feel alive. I possibly feel more alive in Your nature than I do in the earthly existence I have tried to build on my own. This is as it should be. It is Your pure Creation speaking to another of Your creations. It is so easy to commune with You in this situation. The world in the background and You and Your beauty before me, each thought of You making me even more alive inside.

I cannot go to the ocean without sitting and watching the sun go down over the ocean. There is this majestic light stretching from the sinking sun, reaching out to me across the water surface directly to my line of vision. I can move a distance away from it or in any direction and the light is always reaching out to me--to my line of vision. The only way I can lose sight of the light is to turn away or to shut my eyes to it. The light is still there, I have just temporarily removed myself from the picture.

Oh, Father, how much this is like You. You cast a continual light of eternal salvation in my direction. Your light is always there, just for me. The length of the light and the direction is constant. The only variable seems to be me. Do I look toward the light? Do I stay in the light's path? Or do I turn away at times? We all turn away at times, Father. It is our human nature. You have given the gift of free will, but at times, this "will" does get in the way of the light You are sending. There is a break in the connection.

"Then spake Jesus again unto them, saying, I am the light of the world: he that followeth me shall not walk in darkness, but shall have the light of life." -- John 8:12.

Oh, Father, thank You for continuing to send Your light: the light of Your Word, the light of Your promises, the light of Your Son, Jesus Christ. Of one thing I can be sure, once I became Your child, I always have Your light to illuminate the darkness. All I have to do is to glory in it. Thank You for these reminders of Your faithfulness and love.

I love You.

THE DOCTOR WILL SEE YOU NOW
#1—Where Can I Go?

You're only lost when you don't <u>know</u> where you're going. So ask!

I was sitting in a doctor's office today, Father. There were so many things going on, and I had nothing but time on my mind, so I started to look around. As usual, Your Spirit allowed me to see things which inspired me, comforted me, and made me think of some things I have not taken time to consider before.

The office was what it was created to be: a place where sick people gathered in a common place to find a cure for their illnesses. Some of the people were limping or leaning on crutches. Some were just sitting and staring into space; others were calmly resting with their heads back and their eyes closed. Some were calmly reading.

Some symptoms of illness were obvious and others were very subtle, but the people had one thing in common—they were there to see their doctor.

I thought back to the time I moved to Chico. Finding a doctor's office was not an easy task. I needed to locate an office which I felt would give my family the best care—not the closest or biggest or most convenient, but the best for the purpose of caring for and maintaining my precious family's health. This took a little searching and asking people for their recommendations—but well worth the effort.

I also needed to find an office which I felt deals in the truth, is straight-forward and follows the physician's manual without hesitation. If in doubt, I want him, the doctor, to check it out.

In addition to all of this, the office we needed also had to have an available, well-trained, friendly, hard-working, capable, and dedicated staff. Our physical well-being is dependent on these factors.

This is a lot like finding and going to church, isn't it, Father? In church, people gather in one location, with different problems, trying to find a cure for individual needs. Once a church is found that teaches Your Word, the search for You begins: If You're not there working, a change is in order. When You are found, You are asked to become **the** physician, and You are faithful to accept every patient as Your own: assuming responsibility for eternity.

After You are found, You schedule daily and weekly visits. If wise, all appointments will be kept. Sometimes arrangements are for maintenance. At other times they are for diagnosis—a symptom is described and Your Spirit shows what needs to be fixed.

At times a member takes a friend because that friend hasn't been feeling well and needs to find a new doctor.

But, the most important reason for the visit is to see the "doctor." You, Father, and Christ, are the Great Physicians. What better physician is there than the Creator of our being: You know people inside and out. You, and only You, can fix what is wrong within a heart.

All we have to do is come to You in prayer, tell You our troubles, ask for help, accept Your diagnosis revealed by Your Spirit, read Your instructions given in Your Word, and follow Your directions faithfully. And You have lovingly and thoughtfully given everyone the Physician's assistant, Father, Godly pastors (Thank You again for mine, and please continue to bless him and his family): These "special" people are available and responsible for nurturing our spiritual growth.

I pray we are as wise and prudent in selecting a church and staff—who will be responsible for the care of our souls—as we are in selecting our doctor's office for the care of our health needs. It is **eternally** more important. Thank You, Father, for Your promise: "... *and, lo, I am with you alway, even unto the end of the world. Amen.*" --Matthew 28:20

It is reasonable to deduce "Where Can I go, but to my Lord."

I love You.

THE DOCTOR WILL SEE YOU NOW
#2—He's My Doctor?
He Takes Good Care of Me!

God is my heart specialist.

Yesterday, Father, many thoughts crossed my mind while visiting my doctor's office. I have already shared some of them with you: We talked about my process of finding a doctor's office. Once I found the office which met my needs, I found a physician and asked him to become my doctor. Once this was done, I became his patient; I am faithful to him and pay him his due. He, in turn, is available to me, prescribes for me, and takes care of my physical needs.

In addition to our previous conversation, Father, I observed that some of the patients were there for follow-up visits. If they follow the doctor's directions, they will likely improve.

Follow-up visits are an important part of a health "routine." I also come to You, Father, for follow-up visits. You tell me in Your Word that You want me to be faithful in following Your instructions. You want to see me come back and want to see if I have made progress or if I am still the same or if I have (God, please forbid) regressed.

While in the doctor's office, I saw some of the people go to the laboratory for tests. A specific illness needed to be found so a cure could be initiated. I am tested, Father, right? That's part of being mortal: I don't have control over my environment and very little control over myself. These tests show what I am made of. They will also give evidence of an illness within me. This is when I need the physician to step in and prescribe for me.

You, as the Great Physician, have not only left instructions for me to follow, but have also given me my Pastor to assist in the treatment. If I let him, he can examine the facts and prescribe from Your Word. I ***must*** follow those instructions. I have had Your instructions ever since I started coming to You, but I may not have followed what You have prescribed, and my Pastor can help me get back on track or to understand where I went wrong.

You tell me in Your Word about three types of illnesses: sickness unto death, as in Your timing for our death. This we can't question because You know what is best for Your children and You are omnipotent.

Another sickness is sickness unto chastisement such as plagues and sicknesses in Your Word given as chastisement for disobedience of Your people. This sickness is a warning. I need to heed and to evaluate my life and make changes when necessary. You have given me my Pastor to help.

The last sickness is sickness unto Your glory such as in the "death" of Lazarus. *"When Jesus heard that, he said, This sickness is not unto death, but for the glory of God, that the Son of God might be glorified thereby."* --John 11:4

This last sickness is when I'm allowed to see Your miracles of healing. I have witnessed Your Miracles, Father. Every day of life with You is a miracle: I experience aspects of Your personal Glory which are beyond my understanding. This is where faith comes in, isn't it? I do have faith in You, Father, and in Jesus Christ and the Holy Spirit.

I pray I will always faithfully pay toward my debt. I know I will not be able to pay what is due You, but by Your Grace, I will obey Your instructions and do my best.

I love You.

WHEELCHAIRS AND WISDOM
#1 From Growing Pains to Physical Pain

It took a whole book to list God's credentials.

Father, it is so awesome that if You have a lesson for me to learn or a joy to share with me, You teach me by using practically anything within my sight.

I was watching a lady in a walker going up an incline and attempting to enter the door to an office. Someone did come to her assistance; she was appreciative and was able to continue on her way because of that help. This incident caused me to think about the stages of life and how this incident corresponds at times with physical and spiritual lives.

As youth, we walked or ran without thinking twice about it. We didn't hurt; we didn't get winded; we didn't faint from weakness; we were totally unaware of anything outside of our own personal world.

In our spiritual life, before Christ, we, likewise, are independent and unaware of needing any "outside" help. We fell down and got up on our own power, but these falls sometime left bruises and ugly scars. The blessing of strength and health would go unnoticed, but when things went badly for us we sat up and took notice—a lot of tears may also have been involved.

Sometimes during this phase we take on too much independence and get into trouble. We are born into this phase of our lives, though, aren't we, Father? We were born into sin and given free will—but we are also given the promise of a great future (actually an eternity), available to us when we mature.

We eventually progress to the cane/walker phase of our physical lives. We have matured, but acknowledge we need help—it is harder to "go it on our own." We find we have limited mobility—but we can move and function fairly well in a majority of life's situations.

I see this phase much like a new Christian, Father; we look for help, find Christ, accept Him as our Lord and Savior and accept His help. At this point, however, it is all new and we have limited knowledge of the workings of our new power: God the Father, God the Son, and God the Holy Spirit. We have a hard time asking for this new-found help because this dependency is new to us, and we're not certain of how to ask. We must learn how our new help works, how to avoid problem areas, and when to ask for help.

In this phase of our Christian life, we also slow down in our personal life. We put in more thought than we did when we "lived in the fast lane." While we still move under our own power, we don't rely as much on self as we used to. Instead, we call on You, Father. We are still doing too much of our own thing. But, we are moving forward as long as we are seeking Your knowledge.

Another thought—people who use canes or walkers, say they were self-conscious in the beginning because of the change in their lives. They weren't as comfortable around old friends as they were before. This is the same as in our spiritual lives. When we become Christian, we may not feel as comfortable around our old "gang" as we used to. Our friends can become confused and question the changes. The new Christian must let friends know of the change and the differences which must come about. Some friends will understand and others will not. Real friends need to know our mind and heart and respect changes brought about by our new person in Christ.

You help us get over self, Father. When we become Christians we find that we need help--Your help. We have difficulties at first, but, by relying on You, we find that You help us through it all. We become stronger and learn Your ways of doing things. When we fall, You, again, pick us up and heal the wounds. You take the pain away, Father, thank You, and praise Your Name.

I love You.

WHEELCHAIRS AND WISDOM
#2 Pain Relief

*Choose the driver who will take you
where you <u>know</u> you <u>should</u> go.*

Father, I am still thinking of lessons that I can learn from mobility devices. Earlier today I shared with you thoughts about the stages of life from childhood to reliance on canes and walkers. I shared my thoughts about reliance on You. My thoughts have now progressed to consider the use of a wheelchair.

A wheelchair is the next logical step to fight our weakness; it is still powered by self. We do, however, find it takes less of our own strength and we begin to rely on the strength of the "tool." With this wonderful tool, some of the weakened parts of the body are not used as much as they once were, but other parts are exercised more than before.

This made me think of a Christ-"driven" person. We still function as an individual and everything remains as it was before: we still sin, but we are now forgiven. We have Christ who carries the weight of our sin and the burdens of life. Sin is still present, hardship is still present, but we rely on Your faithfulness and love to get us over the tough spots. The weakened area of our life we have turned over to You. We now have started to exercise our spiritual areas of our new life through You. What a joy!

As with walkers, it is still difficult to go up the hills—we need help at times to get up the steep areas. When things are not easy, we have Your power, Christ's attributes, and the Holy Spirit's attributes to call upon to get over the rough spots, and, thank You, Father, that You don't give us more than we can bear. You will give us the physical and emotional strength necessary when we need it, and You provide the help required for the task ahead—and a little push once in a while doesn't hurt either.

A wheelchair is, however, hard to turn around without help. If we are headed in the wrong direction, we could need help in turning it around. We can rely on You, Father, to turn our lives around and head us in the proper direction. This is the start of freedom: freedom from the bondage of sin. The assurance is that the help is always there for our asking.

The ultimate tool for carrying a weak person is a motorized wheelchair. I delight in thinking of this as a "motorized" Christian. This is a totally God-powered life--it has all of the bells and whistles without leaving anything out: loving kindness, faithfulness, eternal salvation, shelter in the time of need, and family.

We don't need to rely on our own strength, because You are there—all the time. Your strength is always there when we ask for it. Your strength flows through us. Freedom returns: freedom is again obtained, only through a different source: the burdens have been lifted, the wounds healed, the pain removed, and the direction has been set. We just need to learn to let You pilot our lives.

Even with a wheelchair or motorized chair, we do find that doors are still a problem, Father. We need You always to open the doors we should enter and to close the doors we should not approach. Father, I thank You for opening the gates of heaven for eternity.

I love You.

WHAT I LOVE ABOUT MY CHURCH

A jar is a jar is a jar—but,
to be a cookie jar it has to have cookies.

Today was "I Love My Church" Sunday at my church, Father. Why do I love my church? What is a church? These were questions that were asked by Pastor. That's why we're talking now, Father, I want to share my blessing with You.

Oversimplified, a "church" is an assembly of people with common spiritual beliefs. It isn't necessarily a building. Many churches were started out in the open—in Your Creation. It could be an assembly of believers held in the proposed parking lot of a proposed building. It could be in the woods. It could be anywhere. It is the purpose of the gathering and the belief that makes it a church. It is people—ordinary people—with an extraordinary desire to search for You and to please You.

Why? It starts with love, Father—love of You, love of Your Word, love of country, love of family, love of friends, and love of brothers and sisters in Christ. Oh, and, Father, my church loves me. With me, I love, in the right way, Pastor and his family (thank You, again, Father, for them). I love our deacons and church staff; they work so hard and with such energy and devotion. I love my pew partners. I love the friendly faces, the eager prayer warriors, the helpful hands, the callers, the soul winners, the discipleship warriors, and the visitors.

I love my church, Father, because it is a working church and You are there. I feel Your presence when I am listening to the sermon. When I leave, I feel as though I have been to church. Pastor's words ring true and are from Your Word. Not his words, Father, but Your Words to us. We get the whole story and none is held back.

A good pastor loves Your children, his flock. Our pastor does. He shows it in his diligence to serve You and his diligence to teach us Your Word. Love gives warning, admonishments, chastisements, and all of the benefits of a loving relationship. A loving parent doesn't let the child do something harmful without giving the consequences of a wrongful action. This admonishment is then followed through with a loving, appropriate counsel—like the way You admonish us for our sin and then help us.

You are everything, Father. You are all dimensional. So many Christians today have a one-sided God: they acknowledge Your blessings and miracles, as should be taught by all churches, Father, but they forget that there is also judgment to consider. Something is wrong with that picture. You tell us in Your Word that there is judgment, and that we are all going to face that moment.

Thank You, Father, for a church that teaches me the difference between right and wrong and gives me the whole story. A Biblical church is a rare blessing that should be preserved at all cost and sought after with all diligence. Father, please grant me the grace to be steadfast in prayer for Your churches and Your leaders.

I love You.

COFFEE TIME

*Begin your day with God;
end it with thanksgiving*

    I love mornings, Father—not quite as early morning as I did in my younger years, but mornings. They are a time for our family to visit, set our schedules, see if anyone needs anything, and top it off with "that" morning cup of coffee. It's not the coffee itself, Father. I would even enjoy this time without the coffee.

    Coffee time is a relaxing, quiet way to ease into the day ahead. It consists of "Good morning!" "I love you!" "What kind of a night did you have?" "How are you doing?" "What are you going to do today?" "You did a 'super' job yesterday, thank you!" "Is there anything I can do for you today?" "I need help with **something or other**." "I need to share this with you." "I need to do **such and such**; how would you do it?" "A friend needs help with **this or that**, would you please help her." It is a stimulating time, a loving time, and a time that sets the tone for our activities.

    I enjoy my coffee time—without the coffee—with You, Father. I call it my "quiet time," and it is the best way to start my day. It wakes me up; it is stimulating; it is a loving visit; and it sets the tone for my personal existence during the day. In my "coffee time" with You, I get to greet You, tell You that I love You, tell You how truly wonderful You are, and, again, thank You for all that You did for me the day before.

    It is also a time to thank You for caring for me during the night. It is a time for me to glory in Your new day—and to pray that I don't waste it. My quiet time with You is a time to visit with You in prayer and to search Your Word for answers and absolutes. All I need to do is to listen with my heart and the Spirit will do the rest. You always listen and You are always available. This is a time for me to drink in Your presence, instead of drinking coffee. (Coffee lasts for a couple of hours, Father, but Your presence lasts forever—there is no contest.)

Quiet time is a time to ask You what I can do for You. I tell You about things which delight me, confuse me, concern me, and alarm me. I ask You, "What do I do about them?" "What can I say to her?" "Does someone need my help; how can I help them?"

This is a time for me to share with You the things I am having difficulty doing and to find out from You how I should do them--or turn them over to You and Your infinite powers to accomplish when it is time to let go and let You take the lead.

My time with You is a time to reflect on the day ahead: a time to plan with You. It is a time to share requests for help for people I know or even those whom I don't know, but am aware of a need. You want us to pray for others. You tell us to present our prayers and supplications to You—whatever is on our hearts.

This is a time to pray about the needs of Pastor, staff, volunteer church workers, missionaries, and all of the missions of my church. Not blanket requests, Father, but fervent, heartfelt prayers by name and need.

Finally, Father, this is a time to lose myself in Your Word. Thank You for giving me such a glorious "coffee time." With You, it is, indeed, the most beneficial part of my day.

I love You.

BURDENS AND EXPECTATIONS

Just keep asking. God wants to know if you're serious.

Father, I want to share something funny with You. You know Max II, the big, wonderful cat that You sent Mom after she lost the first Max and prayed for another pet to love. He is a delight for all of us, thank You. Max II became diabetic and had to go on a strict diet. (He didn't like this at all—could it be that he is a little spoiled?) Well, Max did something unusual—even for him—these past *two* nights. We **kept** (past tense) a loaf of bread on the kitchen counter; it was easy for us to get it when **we** wanted it. Max jumped up on the counter, picked up that loaf of bread by the sealed end, and carried it, banging against his little chest for the full length of the house to Mom's room. He then jumped up on the bed (with the loaf of bread) at 5 a.m., gently laid the loaf by Mom's side, and sat there looking in her eyes (she says, "with a look of expectation").

This situation was humorous, Father; however, in relating it to the human condition, it isn't so funny. This situation is the same as with many of us: we end up where we shouldn't be, have what we shouldn't have, disobey, and get into trouble. After all of this, we then bring our burden to You, looking to You, in expectation, to "feed" us. These are generally self-inflicted wounds. We know that as long as we follow Your Word, seek Your counsel, and listen in the quiet for Your answer or search Your Word for the answer, we will be just fine. But, we step "outside," and then we end up coming to You to bail us out. Why didn't we come to You first?

Father, some people carry their burden for such a long time. Some people wear their burden like a badge. Others realize that they do not have to carry the burden, so they turn it over to You. They realize that if they did carry the burden then they would be unable to help someone else because their own burden would keep getting in the way.

You are an awesome God and Father to pull us out of trouble time and time again with love. You are so faithful with Your love for us. As you tell me, again, Father, *"It is of the Lord's mercies that we are not consumed, because his compassions fail They are new every morning: great is thy faithfulness."*

-- Lamentations 3: 22-23.

Father, You already know that Mom took some of the bread out and fed Max a couple of small pieces. When we lay our burden at Your feet, You forgive us, confirm Your love for us, and feed our hunger, sooth our pains, or heal our wounds.

Father, thank You so very much that You are always there for us and do what is best for us. We can come to You with an expectation of answered prayer. We must realize, however, that prayer is **always** answered, but sometimes that answer is **NO**. We don't know why, at times, but we know You do know and that it is Your **Will** based on Your Power, and that is more than sufficient.

I love You.

FREE FOR THE ASKING

Reading material is a source of mental nutrition
Again, choose wisely.

We have two senior citizen publications in Chico, Father. I love to read one of them because it is designed with me, and people like me, in mind. It is designed for a specific audience and designed to meet the needs, interests, and desires of its readers.

I can thumb through this little paper to learn about specific actions that I can take for certain maladies. It tells me how to do things, with the implied message that it's never too late, and that death is the only thing that can keep me from accomplishing whatever "it" is. The monthly paper contains information about nature, food, and recipes. It has articles on history, ideas, and travel. It contains ads, coupons, classifieds, and warnings. All in one cover and new every month—AND IT'S FREE.

This little magazine caused me to consider Your Word, Father, the Holy Bible. It is designed for **all** people, not just a select group. It is available to all, browsed through by some, and whole-heartedly read time-and-time again by others. As the Spirit leads, it is new every reading. The Spirit is available daily, Father, not monthly.

The Bible is custom-designed for needs, interests, and the desires of its audience—any audience. It has remedies for all human maladies. It tells how to become Yours with the message that the door is always open; however, when the door shuts in death, it's too late. It reminds me that because I ask for redemption before my death, death leads me to a glorious world I cannot even imagine because it is beyond my human understanding.

I was led to consider the contents of the Bible compared to the contents of my little monthly publication. The Bible also contains articles about *nature*: the creation, the carnal nature of man, the spiritual nature of redeemed man, all creatures and their natures, the earth in the beginning, and the interactions of human beings.

The Bible also contains references to *food*: The bread of life, the living waters, manna from heaven, salt, and many others. It contains *recipes* on how to build a new life, how to add spice to my life, what things I should be mixed up in, and what things do not mix well with a Christian life.

Your Word has books of history, law, love, poetry, "how to," travel, and it even has a book about the future. It tells about the history of mankind: past, present, and future. The travel chapters tell me of global and spiritual travels: preparations, what to do when I get there, and what to look out for. When I travel, I can pack a whole library in my suitcase—all wrapped up in one cover.

Coupons? Well, no. I don't have to have a coupon. Redemption is for the asking. Salvation is by grace! It doesn't get better than that. The high price has already been paid by Christ.

There are even classifieds in the Bible. The classifieds which stand out in my mind are: WANTED: Workers for the Field. WANTED: Shepherds for the Flocks. WANTED: Good and Faithful Servants. WANTED: Children to live with Me in My home in Paradise.

Father, I thank You for these delightful thoughts. What a joy they bring. My Bible will always guide me through a better life, and combined with prayer and the presence of the Holy Spirit, delights unnumbered are at my fingertips—AND THE BENEFITS ARE FREE FOR THE ASKING!

I love You.

HAPPY ANNIVERSARY

Its easy to say "I do."
But when he's gone, can I say, "I did."

My sister and brother-in-laws' 50th wedding anniversary is coming up next month, Father.

An anniversary is such a special time: a time of celebration, a time of memories, and a time of sharing. Anniversaries are also times that mark important events in our lives. We dare not forget them. They are used to remind us of worthy sacrifice and to remind us of life-changing events.

We have celebrated our country's Bicentennial; we remember Pearl Harbor Day, Memorial Day, 9-11, and many other of our country's anniversaries, reminding us of sacrifice and honor—lest we forget. We celebrate birthdays and anything else we want to remember--or that would be a disservice to forget.

We celebrate more anniversaries than we consciously think of—events which meet the requisites of an anniversary. The first which comes to my mind is the anniversary of a birth. We call them birthdays. They are a time to celebrate a birth, the time we have had with the person, the love we have for them, and the events which have happened throughout the years—memories.

Other anniversaries occur at various times throughout our lives. We celebrate our wedding day every year to remember years of love, laughter, and tears together. The key word here is "together."

We have anniversaries at work. These are seniority celebrations: five years, ten years, fifteen years, and on and on until retirement. These are celebrations of service to a company and celebrating the friendships and changes which have occurred throughout the years.

We put flowers on graves of loved ones for special occasions or on Memorial Day for respect and memorial for those deserving honor. Father, these are all important to us in our earthly existence. We need to honor and remember worthy service, sacrifice, and events.

Praise You, Father, that we can add a few more to our list of true celebrations of life-changing events. Thank You for Jesus Christ, born into a world of sin, but not being tarnished by it: living the perfect life as an example for us to follow. Praise You, Father for *Christmas*.

Thank You, Father, for giving us Jesus Christ who died on the cross to pave the way to eternity for us. It is only fitting that we should celebrate the day of deliverance: *Easter*—a season of honor and glory to Your Son, and to the Lord God Almighty.

Thank You, Father, for giving us pastors and soul winners to lead us to Your saving grace. We should celebrate the anniversary of our *salvation* and receiving the promise of eternal life with You in heaven. Please let us always remember the date of our second birth.

Thank You, Father, for our churches and the freedom to become members of a Christian fellowship. Our years of *membership* are worthy anniversaries and should be celebrated.

These are all important events, Father, life-changing events. If You were to ask me when these anniversaries are, would I be embarrassed for not making "big" of them or for forgetting the dates? Thank You, for the life-changing, honor-worthy anniversaries which come into my life.

I love You.

A BEAUTIFUL BOUQUET OF FLOWERS

God's sweet Spirit needs sharing.

As we discussed earlier, Father, Mom and I start our spring mornings on the back patio—Bill joins us a little later for conversation. After we wake up a little, we "survey the kingdom" that You have given us. It is a constant surprise and delight to see what You have added from one day to the next. One day we have a few little pieces of green showing, and the next morning we have beautiful blossoms. Today we surveyed "the kingdom" and found flowers which are leftovers from two or three years ago. What a joy.

On the west side of our yard, Mom has planted a beautiful variety of plants. They are of different foliages, different colors, different life spans, different needs, and different sizes—all different, but giving equal happiness. We have pansies, stocks, hostas, caladiums, alyssum, hyacinths, azaleas, and primroses—all in a big planter Bill and his brother Bob made specifically for Mom's needs. The garden rests under a beautiful tulip tree. Its large, hovering branches give the flowers a welcomed break from the heat; yet, it yields to the sun so the light and warmth will stimulate growth and blossoming.

I was blessed to look at the garden and think of my church and my church family. A church family is a lot like the garden, isn't it, Father? A bouquet of souls firmly rooted in a common belief—a belief in You. We come to Your garden from different backgrounds. We are of different color, of different life span, different need and different size. The differences add to the beauty and make it more exciting.

As the tree does for Mom's flowers, Your outstretched arms shelter Your children from harm. You not only provide a shade of protection, but You gave us Your Son, the Light of the world, to care for us and give us eternal life; You provide us with Your Word which feeds us. Christ sent us the Holy Spirit to help us grow. And You provide a local body of believers from whom we gain warmth.

While considering this, another thought occurred to me to ponder: It is amazing that the heart of the flower always reaches for the sun. The sun is steadfast in direction and the flower conforms to the direction of the sun—the sun does not conform to the flower. This, truly, is as it should be: Again, Your Word must not conform to our lives, but we must conform our lives to Your Word.

Thank You so very much for Your beautiful flowers, for my thoughts about You. Thank You for my wonderful family. Thank You for my church family, welcoming more "flowers" into Your garden. We are all flowers who need Your cooling shade of protection and Your Son.

Praise you, Father. My heart will always reach for Your Son.

I love You.

WHEN I BECOME OLD(ER)

One age may compliment another age—but, complements never age.

Life is so wonderfully planned, Father. You don't do anything halfway. That fact in itself should be a lesson for me.

I was considering a group of people the other day. They were of every possible description, but what impressed me were the differences among the age groups. There were children, teens, young adults, adults, and seniors. In this case, the seniors were senior saints. What a blessing!

These *children* are from the age groups of babies to intermediates. They need to be guided and they need special care, but all are precious to their parents. They are still in what I call the spoon-feeding stage of life. (Not literally, but figuratively speaking—but You know that.)

The *teens* show excitement in everything: exuberant, energetic, and curious. They are learning everything they can, some of it good, some not so good. They are in a learning period of their life and still in need of guidance.

To me, the *young adult* represents inexperienced application. They are applying what they know. They are totally self-sufficient (speaking of human capability), but are still gaining experience through life, counseling, application and study.

The *adults* at gatherings are sought after by the young adults when advice or help is needed. The mature adult represents, to me, experienced living. Life teaches many lessons which cannot be learned in any other way.

The final group I thought about was the senior saints. They are patient, loving, and experienced beyond their years. In this particular group, I noticed the influence that they had over the other groups at this gathering. This group of saints had not only matured in life, in learning, in application, and in love, but had also matured in their spiritual lives. They are mentors - earning, deserving, and receiving respect. These seniors are "givers," not takers. They observe with knowing eyes, they admonish with compassionate lips, they advise with understanding, and they interact with loving hearts.

Thank You, Father, so very much, for such an honorable, Godly assemblage of saints. They counsel with truth from Your Word; they help however and whomever they can; they serve whenever and wherever they can. They become "adopted" parents, grandparents, older brothers or sisters, or whatever role needs to be filled in a life. They accept trials with praise, patience, dignity, and faith in You. They never retire; they courageously move on to different endeavors.

Many of the saints have moved to Your Kingdom, Father. They are with You. What better ending to a good life. Other saints are slowing down and showing their age—not in attitude, compassion, love, devotion, or other areas in which they excel, but in body.

Father, grant me the grace to cherish these dear people while I have the opportunity to learn from them. I'm a senior myself; however, I have a lot to learn from those who are older, wiser, and willing to share. Grant me the grace to grow old graciously as these dear saints, and while I mentor others, apply what Your Word, Your shepherd, and Your saints have taught me.

I love You.

PROBLEMS, POTHOLES, AND PRAISE

*If you know there's a pothole ahead,
don't aim for it.*

Father, today is Your day. Our Pastor (thank You, again, for Pastor and his family) spoke to us from the text of II Samuel 17: 1-11: the wonderful story of David and Goliath. What a magnificent example of Your power (available to us just by asking) to overcome seemingly insurmountable odds. As Pastor said—in application—if we overcome the seemingly impossible situation, life gets better. If, on the other hand, we let the problem defeat us, we will be a slave to it forever. Those who do not call on Your Power are limited to solutions within human bounds. For those who believe in Your unending Power, it is available for solutions beyond human capability. Problems will always exist. We so many times focus on the problem rather than the solution, and the sooner we realize that You are the solution—in whatever way You will—life becomes easier.

Pastor spoke to us, likening problems in life to potholes in a road. Once a person hits the pothole, he or she is aware of its existence and its location and looks for ways to avoid hitting it, again. This indicates to me that there is much that can be done to avoid personal problems. There are no new problems—someone else has gone or is going through the same thing.

If I don't pay attention to the path on which I'm traveling, I may suffer by hitting the potholes. It is not Your will that I hit them, but by my doing or not doing I seem to find them. Yet, like any child, I will come to You, Father, only after the fact for help; and You, again, tell me to keep on the path and everything will be all right.

While considering the potholes that Pastor talked about, I thought about some other holes that can appear in lives. These aren't problems understandable to the observer. The person going through it is not really aware that anything in *particular* is wrong. He or she feels incomplete, uneasy, and vacant in existence. There is a void which needs to be filled and there is just no getting around it because it is not always visible. These voids might be caused by the loss of a loved one or a sudden, unexpected change in life—or the cause can be totally unknown or unexplainable. It is just known that something is not right.

Father, everyone experiences periods of void in life. It isn't apparent what is wrong, but something is definitely not right: It's an empty feeling. We are anxious. We could be jittery. And, we definitely are uneasy inside. It is one of those troubling winds that blow.

Yet You have always seen Your children through these times. When I go through these times, I start out by asking for Your calm because I don't have any of my own. I usually sing a good, **old** hymn: the words are reassuring to me and they seem to put things into perspective. I search Your Word for solutions, Father, and as usual, I end up at Philippians 4:6-8. We've talked about this passage before. Oh, Father, Your Word has the solutions. It just takes turning pages, reading, and asking for answers to whatever it is that is troubling me. To my chagrin, I generally find that the Spirit convicts me of something which has taken my eyes off of the road.

You are the solution to the voids and potholes in my life. You fill up the void with Your love, Your promises, and the joy of the Spirit. The price for this service was paid for by Christ. Praise You for Your everlasting goodness. Whatever the cause or whatever the outcome, You help me overcome the seemingly insurmountable. You are good—all the time.

I love You.

BUDS, BLOSSOMS, AND FRUIT

Buds and children need the right exposure before showing fruit.

I went to an office, Father, and as I approached the front door of the office, I saw a beautifully landscaped walkway of flowering trees: mock cherry trees to be exact. I know this is not a "real" fruit tree; however, it reminded me of the orchards that we have in our beautiful area: almonds, peaches, apricots, figs, cherries, and many, many more fruitful trees. We are so blessed.

I thought of how the fruit trees bud. The buds will soon become blossoms. The bees will come and pollinate the blossoms and then, weather permitting, the trees will bear fruit. What a wonderful evolving of blessings. The buds are a hope and expectation of the things to come.

The blossoms fill my eyes with beauty as I enjoy their colors—and, again, the promise of fruit. And then, Oh, Father, the wonderful fruit to refresh, satisfy, and delight, filling my heart with rejoicing and praise.

This whole process is dependent upon the weather. If the weather is good, everything goes along as necessary for a fruitful harvest. If the weather is inclement, the orchards do not yield as much fruit as originally expected, the cost of fruit rises, and the quality of what little fruit comes is, in many cases, unacceptable.

You talk many times in Your Word about budding trees and fruit. Every Word from Your mouth is important, Father, but when You mention something more than once, I consider it as something absolutely significant or vital—something to be pondered.

You mentioned the budding of Aaron's rod in Numbers 17:8. This was a miraculous sign for the children of Israel, but it was and is also a sign of resurrection: life from death. You also talked about a fig tree which did not produce fruit for Your Son, so it withered and died.

Is this me, Father? Am I unproductive? I pray not. Is my fruit acceptable? I pray it is. You provide the necessary nurturing elements through Your Word and through Your shepherds. Do I let the stormy days of life keep me from blossoming? I pray not. Do I let the frost of indifference interfere with my witnessing? I pray not.

We are all as fragile as the small blossoms which are blown in the wind or die in a frost. I pray that I can weather the storms of life, blossom as a Christian, and produce fruit for Your Kingdom. I also pray, Father, that my works—from the heart—and my obedience to Your Word be like flowering trees of love blossoming for You—especially when they bear fruit.

I paused to think of the saying "Bloom where you're planted." Oh, Father, please purpose me to accept this as my personal prayer and let me bloom for You wherever I am—geographically, physically, or emotionally.

I love You.

UMBRELLAS 101

Ask God to customize your protection.

An umbrella is such a marvelous invention, Father. Once opened, it will do the job required. When I close it, I'm no longer protected from the storm. The imperative thing about an umbrella is that I do have to open it if I want its shelter.

Some umbrellas have cute little pictures or decorative designs on them. Some are just plain. Some umbrellas are large enough to shelter more than one person, and other umbrellas are just the right size to protect children. Whatever the use, need, or desire, they can be found.

The important thing about umbrellas is that they give a cover of protection when shelter is needed. They keep the rain off; they keep the cold and damp of the snow away, and they can also keep the sun from blistering or burning.

There are so very many uses for the umbrella. When someone nearby needs an umbrella, we can offer ours. It is a good thing to share with those who need protection or are facing personal challenges where protection would be needed.

In Your Word, Father, You tell me about hedges. An umbrella reminds me of Your hedges. (I do know that hedges do go around instead of over, but I am referring to the sheltering aspect of both—but then, You already know that). They are for protection from danger or harm or whatever the need. Perhaps the most important hedge I can pray for someone is the hedge to protect them from evil. Evil is so invasive. It will find an opening in any possible way, but it cannot penetrate wherever You have planted Your hedge of protection.

The hedge, Father, is illustrative of Your protection, isn't it? You tell me of Your protection of Job. Satan asks the question: *"Hast not thou made an hedge about him, and about his house, and about all that he hath on every side? Thou hast* *blessed the work of his hands, and his substance is increased in the land." --*Job 1:10.

Hedges are used throughout Your Word to point out the way of the slothful. What happens when hedges are broken down and the protection is taken away? holy ordinances? heavy judgments? numerous afflictions? You are in charge of all hedges. Some hedges need to be built up and some need to be removed, and some need to be built as reminders.

Oh, Father, You grant requests to build hedges around us and those who are in our prayers. You are with Your missionaries when a hedge is requested to be built around them for their protection and to keep evil away from them and their ministry. Father, we always need to pray for our children that You build a loving hedge of protection around them to protect them from harm and from evil. You are always faithful in building hedges if we are faithful to ask.

Oh, thank You, Father, for Your hedge of everlasting love.

I love You.

MORE THAN THE AVERAGE SIGN

Can you pass your driving test?

Tonight was "Ladies Night Out" at our church, Father. Thank You so very much for each one of Your ladies—they are indeed a blessing to me. This is an evening for ladies of the church to come together just to enjoy each other's company and to go home inspired and refreshed from the gathering. I have talked with You, Father, about the ladies of our church. They are truly my sisters in Christ. We have the same God; we have the same Bible; we have the same spiritual leaders to guide us on the path of righteousness.

The theme for this evening was travel. The games involved travel and travel items as a theme. It was, indeed, a very fun time. We always look forward to the ending of the fun and games time—not that we don't enjoy it, but because we know what comes next. It is like one of my friends said, "I come here for the food and sermon." She was being humorous, but I thought to myself, food for the stomach and food for the soul.

The spiritual exercise for the evening (based upon the theme of travel) was road and travel signs. The leader for the evening asked us to look at the road signs posted around the room and to come up with spiritual meanings for each. It was a most revealing exercise: building a story from a single word or two. I know You have already heard them because they were for Your honor and from the hearts of these dear ladies. *Some of the examples which touched my heart are as follows:*

> ***STOP***
>
> **Stop** and let me tell you what the Lord has done for me.
> **Stop** and think before doing wrong.
> **Stop** before something unpleasing to God escapes your lips.
> **Stop** hesitating.

SLOW:
> **Slow** down and count your blessings.
> **Slow** down and be sure before continuing on.

SCHOOL XING: (Children educated in a Christian school with Godly teachers and with parents backing the educators are such blessings.)
> **Study** the Word. **Teach** your children the important things.

YIELD
> **Yield** not to temptation.
> **Yield** to the Lord.

BICYCLE XING:
> (When one rides a bicycle, they go uphill as well as downhill. This is the same as in life: life has its ups and downs. When necessary, change to a bicycle built for two and ask God to go along with you to help when you don't have the strength to do it on your own.)
>
> (When a person rides a bicycle, they have the appearance of calm on top, but they are pedaling like crazy beneath. When we have the calm of the Spirit, we can remain calm even though things are still churning inside.)

CAUTION:
> **Caution,** there is always something out there trying to make you detour. Don't detour from the straight path.

NO U-TURN:
> **No U-Turn**--Once you become a Christian, there is no turning back. You may hit detours along the way of life, but just look toward the Lord and follow His directions to get back on the main road.

NO WALKING:
> **No Walking**--We are in a race to the end.

RESTRICTED:
>(They are commandments, not suggestions. We have freedom of choice, but, according to Your Word, not all things are beneficial and some are on the restriction list.)

REST STOP:
>**Stop and rest** in the Word.

NO PARKING:
>**No Parking.** There's time for rest and for slumber, but no time for stopping. God's work must continue.

RESERVED PARKING:
>(Heaven is reserved for God's Children.)

MEN WORKING:
>**Men Working** 'til the night is over."
>
>Where man works for God, the improvements are unlimited and beyond hopes and dreams.

NO VEHICLES BEYOND THIS POINT:
>You can't take it with you. The trip to heaven is by private transport only.

ROAD CLOSED:
>**Road Closed** to certain places and activities if you're a Christian. The **road** to heaven is never closed to His children.

NO DETOUR:
>The **road** to heaven is through Jesus Christ. There are no **detours**.

DO NOT ENTER—WRONG WAY:
>**Do not enter** into temptation.
>
>**Do not enter** into dangerous areas—keep geographically grounded. Geographic dislocation (going to the wrong type of place, going down the wrong aisle in a grocery store, etc.) can lead to temptation.

ROAD WORK AHEAD—
God is still working on us and working in us. We must follow the directions of the "flagman." Slow down, and follow directions.

You spoke to us multiple times in Your Word of signs, Father. Why shouldn't we accept earthly signs which lead us to thoughts of You, as well as to expect spiritual signs to speak to us of earthly duty and behavior.

Father, this has been so exciting for me; I will never look at road signs the same way again. They will have a much larger meaning for me. And when I travel, You, as well as the authority of government, will direct me. Thank You for this, another blessing.

I love You.

LOST IN THE EMPTY WELL

*When you meet yourself coming back,
you may have missed half of the trip.*

It's been a hard two weeks, Father. It doesn't make any sense to be lost in an empty well, does it? The sides are all around me and there is only one way out. How could anyone become lost? But that's what it has been like these past two weeks—it didn't make sense. Have I been running around in circles and not looking up? We've talked before about the holes in our lives. I know I'm not the only woman who has felt this way:

I wasn't interested in anything; I was without inspiration; and, the worst thing of all, I wasn't able to pray anything except "Thank You, Father" over and over again. As a pastor told me long ago, look first to the physical. This is generally my signal of a physical challenge, so I visited my doctor. He prescribed something and took care of the physical difficulty; however, the emotional void remained. I know, for me, the only way to get out of the depths is to look up—the well was dry.

I finally decided to look up, Father. I shut myself in my quiet room and got on my knees. You were still there, I just needed to look in the right direction and approach it from the ground level. What did I do, if anything? What was I to pray for? I know that if I reach out to You, You will meet me there I didn't know what was wrong, so I prayed to You for forgiveness for sins I was unaware of, asked for answers, and then listened for conviction of what those things might be. In listening in the quietness, Father, thank You for letting me know what I needed to get right.

Thank You for answered prayer and for the working of the Holy Spirit. I realized that I was trying to pump from an empty well: there wasn't anything there and it was drastically in need of replenishing. You did, indeed, replenish and left me with my cup running over—not just full, but running over. Thank

You, Father. You pulled me from the depths and brought me back into the sunshine, as usual.
    I love You.

HAIR TODAY, BUT GONE TOMORROW

A Christian's beauty comes from the inside.

My friend did my hair today, Father. We are leaving for a trip and I **needed** a perm—vanity, all is vanity. In today's society, people have their hair "done" for many reasons. You know **my** feeble excuses for self-indulgent behavior: my hair needs cleaning, a change of style, a trimming, or a major cut. So I visited someone who knows what she's doing.

I don't go to someone who does not know how to recognize and deliver what I need. Notice, Father, that I didn't say what I want. Sometimes what I want and what I need are two different things—what I want may not necessarily be what is best for me. You, Father, are all-knowing. You know what I need, and it would be an abomination to question Your decisions.

As regards my hair, Deborah may counsel me, but the choice is mine, good or bad. I am wise when I listen to her counsel and allow her to do what is in my best interest. I feel so good when my hair is done—I feel better about myself. I feel that I represent myself and my family better when I at least look well-groomed.

In retrospect, as with my hair, my choices in life affect my ministry; they also cast a reflection of Your Kingdom. I pray it is a clear, Godly reflection and not an unclear, confusing one.

Others look at me differently when I have my hair fixed—they notice a difference when I change styles. When I have my hair "done" I feel like a new person.

This makes me think of us when we accept Christ as Savior. We become a new person, and others do notice the change. Some changes are small. Others, in comparison, are gigantic in nature because of what the Spirit helps overcome. Many times the change inspires others to look for a change for themselves. This is witnessing, Father, witnessing for You. I do have the ability, don't I, Father, through the working of the Spirit, to witness and to inspire others. I have the ability with the Spirit's guidance to direct others to the One, Jesus Christ, who can work miracles in the inner appearance to show an outer example of faith and love.

As a new Christian, we are given a new beginning—a fresh start, much like a shaved head. As a shaved head gives access to the sun and allows a fresh beginning, Your Son, Jesus Christ, has complete access to our hearts which allows fresh growth and change. Oh, Father, what a wonderful thought—we do have access also to You and to Your Son. Our beloved Donnie was one of Your children who had Your Son shine on him throughout his short life. He did not hide it. What better legacy could he leave his family.

Father, You know I love my church—we've talked about it many times. I have been to some churches that are like wigs: they cover the surface, but there are no roots. I love my church, Father, because it is rooted in Your Word. We need to remember that today we have hair to be concerned about, but tomorrow **we** could be gone.

Here I am having my hair done for a trip, but have I made adequate preparations for the most important journey of my life? I am assured that I have, but I may need to get rid of some baggage I've collected along the way. Thank You, Father, for your goodness and Grace which is sufficient and grooms me for eternity with You.

I love You.

HAND IN THE COOKIE JAR

Let my speech be flavored with your love.

Father, our friends in Oregon have a cookie jar collection. The jars are so much fun to see. They are of all sizes, shapes, and colors, and they hold a myriad of delights.

These cookie jars don't just mysteriously develop; they are all planned creations made to delight their owners and to be used. It is up to the creator and designer of each to establish the purpose for which it was intended.

It is revealing to consider the cookie jar, Father. Cookie jars are, unfortunately, made of breakable materials. Yet, fortunately, part of their beauty can be found in their fragile and complex make up. We are like them is so many ways. You, our Creator, made each of us unique for Your treasured collection.

Full or empty, the outside of the cookie jar, in general, doesn't change unless something keeps chipping away and weakening the structure. Like them, we can be shattered if we are not handled with care. Thank You, Father, for handling us with care and for keeping us. Because we have been washed in the blood of Christ, You have given us a permanent coating of protection. In order to get rid of the dirt that we have collected along life's way, all we need to do is ask to be "cleansed" so we can, again, be a beautiful creation.

In considering a damaged cookie jar, I, again, thought of the fact that bad things do happen to good people, but You, in all of Your glory and mercy, still have a purpose for us in our weakened physical conditions and treasure us. You simply give us a new mission—much like a cookie jar used by Marge as a vase for a beautiful bouquet of Your flowers.

Cookie jars make wonderful gifts for friends. They are something that we can share with our friends. This allows, in turn, our friends to share the "goodies" inside with others. Your love should be shared like that, Father—from one person to another to another. We have so many "goodies" in us from You that we need to offer them to others. Not everyone will accept what we offer, but we need to offer it and offer it and offer it—You keep our "jar" filled.

Another good thing about Your creation, Father, is that You use others to help keep our "jar" full. You have given us our pastors, our teachers, our mentors, and godly friends to fill us with Your hope and Your sweet Spirit.

One final thought, Father, two people can't put their hands in the jar at the same time without creating problems, can they? We can't serve two masters. You tell us that, in Your Word—in fact, You tell us everything worth knowing and worth living, in Your Word.

Thank You so much, Father, for Your patience in forming us, for Your mercy in keeping us, for Your goodness in filling us with Your bounty of blessings, and for Your love in preserving us for eternity.

I love You.

LOOK OUT FOR THAT DOOR

I'm accountable to you Lord, to "keep on keeping on."

Father, sometimes I feel so awkward. I frequently run into things. If there is a door nearby, I could just as easily walk into it as not. But, there is a lesson available in anything, even my awkwardness.

Doors have a multitude of lessons locked up in their creation. Considering the general construction of doors, I observe that they are generally made of wood: some plain, some fancy, and some become old and weathered. Some other doors have windows to the outside—or inside, depending on where I'm standing at the time. As I move from one side of the door to the other, the view changes.

This reminded me of becoming a Christian. Once I became a Christian, the view changed dramatically: life took on a new glow, and eternity became a welcomed reality.

Doors can open. Gentlemen open doors for ladies, not because the ladies are women, but because the men are gentlemen. They don't have to, but by their thoughtfulness and goodness they do. You, Father, open doors for us by Your Grace. Doors can be opened for me, but I must go through them myself to get to the other side.

Doors also close. Once a door is closed, I can't go through it until it opens again—by whatever means. Some doors are closed so I don't see what is on the other side. Some doors become locked and may never open again, like some doors of opportunity You provide for me. If I don't go through while that door is open, it may be locked to me and may not open again. A blessing lost or an unrecognized answer to prayer may be the cost of delaying.

Father, I pray that I am careful not to close a door on another person. I also pray that I am aware of another's need to have a door held open for them--particularly if they have their "hands full."

Some doors are automatic—they can open simply by approaching them or someone else may open them by going through them before me. The door to eternity was opened for me through Jesus—not by my own power, but by Yours. Yet, again, I must go through it on my own before it closes. Nobody can go through it for me; others can open the door for me, but that is as far as it goes.

Some doors are revolving. If I pay attention, I end up where I want to go. If I don't pay attention, I will keep going around in circles. This is the same as not paying attention to what I'm doing in life. If I don't learn from Your Word, if I don't pay attention to what I know is right, I will just keep repeating the same old mistakes.

I pray that if I should enter a revolving door that I do not interfere with another's progress or get in the way of their destination. I also pray that I don't slow them down or make them go too fast and cause them to fall. And, Oh, Father, please help me not to confuse others.

It's time for praise! I thank You for Your Word and the doors it has opened for me. I thank You for my "garage-door" church which allows me a ***wide*** shield of safety by closing my thoughts to the world and also allows me a place to receive and store Your many blessings. And once the door has been opened to me, it allows me to see the ***big*** picture. Thank You, Father.

I love You.

GATHER ME UP, FATHER
#1 The Dawning

To see a sunrise, you have to wake up.

Father, it is such a joy to watch Your sunrise. We get up early, pack the car for a trip, and start on our way.

We start in the dark and use the artificial lighting of the car to make our way along the highway. It's all right, but it is much better to have the darkness disappear and enjoy the illumination of the sun.

As we proceed along our way toward our destination, there is a faint light which starts to appear from the east. As time passes, the light gets brighter, and soon the sun is completely visible in the sky. WOW! This happens every day: faithfully spreading light, warmth, and cheerfulness on the observer. Thank You for such a daily greeting, Father. I pray I have the good grace to affirm my gratitude to You.

I consciously look for every movement of the sunrise. It thrills me the way the sun rises above the clouds, and soon the beams of the sun pierce the clouds and touch the earth. What a glorious sight--"How Great Thou Art" fills my mind and my heart.

Many things about this scene speak to me of the second coming of Your Son, Jesus Christ. I was born into darkness. When I accepted Christ as my Savior I received and continue to receive warmth, comfort, and life-sustaining power from Him. Since that time, I have been preparing for the trip of a lifetime—eternity, to be exact, and I am watching for Your Son to come down and touch the earth as promised. According to Your Word: *"For as the lightning cometh out of the east, and shineth even unto the west; so shall also the coming of the Son of man be."* --Matthew 24: 27

Your Word tells us of the "real" Son coming—the Light of the world coming in the clouds. Praise You, Father, for this promise of the second coming to gather all of Your children together and establish Your Kingdom.

I love You.

GATHER ME UP, FATHER
#2 Front Row Viewing

*Eternity is a L-O-N-G time.
Where will I spend it?*

We were talking yesterday about the sunrise and the coming of Christ, Father. Scripture tells us: *"Immediately after the tribulation of those days shall the sun be darkened, and the moon shall not give her light, and the stars shall fall from heaven, and the powers of the heavens shall be shaken: and there shall appear the sign of the Son of man in heaven and then shall all the tribes of the earth mourn, and they shall see the Son of man coming in the clouds of heaven with power and great glory. And he shall send his angels with a great sound of a trumpet, and they shall gather together his elect from the four winds, from one end of heaven to the other."* --Matthew 24: 29-31

"And when these things begin to come to pass, then look up, and lift up your heads; for your redemption draweth nigh. Then we which are alive and remain shall be caught up together with them in the clouds, to meet the Lord in the air: and so shall we ever be with the Lord." --Luke 21:28

"For the Lord himself shall descend from heaven with a shout, with the voice of the archangel, and with the trump of God: and the dead in Christ shall rise first. . . ." --1 Thessalonians 4:16

I know Your children will be taken in the rapture, Father, but this is really traveling first-class—with an escort. The sun and all other lights will pale and fade away, giving way to the brightest light of the heavens, Jesus Christ and His heavenly host of angels. Father, I imagine *the* most glorious Son rise of all—even the falling stars providing the fireworks like sun rays reaching the earth.

I imagine darkness on the face of the earth, everyone looking to the heavens—some fearful for they don't know what is coming (or because they do know what is coming and they haven't prepared for it), and others receive the view with awe and glorious anticipation, knowing of the promise to come.

Then, Oh, and then, the Dawn comes with trumpet sounding, angels leading the way, our loved ones who died in Christ rising from the dead, and, finally, the collecting of all of Your children. This is one Son rise we won't want to miss. We've been waiting and watching for it for years: no fear, no darkness, no sickness, no wars, no pain, no more parting—and, no more tribulation. Praise You, Father, for Your eternal plan for Your children.

I love You.

ADOPT-A-HIGHWAY

We don't need an attorney to adopt the right attitude.

I saw an "Adopt-a-Highway" sign the other day, Father. The word "adopt" is a meaningful term to me. Our son was adopted. Notice, Father, he is our son first and adopted strictly as a means of becoming our son. Thank You, Father, for our family.

Adopt means to accept as one's own. It means that, whatever is adopted comes with responsibility. A person should expect results only equal to one's efforts. Adopting a highway holds the same requisites: we find a section we are responsible for, keep it clean, watch it with pride, and let the results of our labor spread joy to ourselves and to others.

When *we* adopt a child, highway, responsibility, or whatever else we choose to adopt, we cannot leave it on its own. We must reach out in order to fulfill our responsibility. With a child, we are very blessed if they come to us, so we need to keep a careful, loving watch over them.

We need to remember that in life, as on the highway, much "trash" comes accidentally or, in some cases, purposefully from people just passing by. We put out "do not litter" signs, but, at times, the signs don't do the job, so we must be diligent. You teach us to be diligent, Father. You teach us to raise a child in the way he should go. You provide one highway, uncluttered and beautiful, leading to You.

Duties for adopting a highway, as well as a child, come in the form of cleaning up, recycling the good to create more good, and discarding or getting rid of the garbage. Oh, Father, we have so much garbage to clean up. We sometimes forget that when we gather too much garbage without sorting through it, it spreads out to the areas of others.

Even Christians have garbage to get rid of, don't we, Father? It can be delivered in attitudes, words, countenance, and actions. Delivery modes misused are no respecters of what is good and right—and they certainly aren't of You. If, however, used properly, words, attitudes, countenance, and actions can clean up a lot of garbage in our world and make it a better place in which to live.

Cleanup isn't accomplished by hiding the garbage, but by actually getting rid of it. This reminds me of the old saying "Don't talk the talk, but walk the walk"—lip service vs. leg service. This cleanup may be the result of an individual effort or of a team effort, such as a discipleship team working in the church. They purpose to help new Christians pick up the pieces of their lives scattered along the way and teach them how to leave a clean path by trusting and relying on You. The new Christians learn how to dispose of garbage as they come across it, and they learn the difference between the good "stuff" and the bad "stuff" according to Your Word—**Your** Word.

Today, Father, there are so many people along the highways of life who are lost, sick, hurting, filthy, needing to sort things out, and needing to be retrieved. Some of them have been accidentally discarded; others have been pushed away or discarded by a society that is oblivious to the needs of others because of their own difficult or cluttered existences. It is so easy to get lost in the world and in needs that we forget the needs of those who are close by us. I pray, Father, that You continually bring to my heart and mind others' needs, particularly their spiritual needs.

Praise You, Father, that some lost along the highway of life will be found, recycled, redeemed, and put on the right road. Thank You, Father, for soul winners and teachers and prayer warriors who have adopted the Highway to heaven to help people, through Your Son Jesus Christ, to pick up the pieces of others' shattered lives. All praise and glory is due to You.

I love You.

OLD DOGS AND NEW LESSONS

Why do you think God put that stranger there? Talk!

Father, You know that when I compare spiritual things to earthly things, I do not mean that one, literally, is like the other. I merely look for applications to my spiritual life. The reason I mention this is because of the unlikely subject of inspiration I received the other day.

While shopping I saw a dog in a car, waiting for its master. The dog's master left everything safe for him and for his comfort, so I wasn't worried about the beautiful creature. But, I started to think about how this incident might have come about—this was fun thinking, thank You.

I visualized, in my mind's eye, the dog wanting to get out of the house to do something different, anything different, for a change in his life. Aren't we like that, Father? As the old saying goes, "the grass is always greener on the other side of the fence."

I also imagined the dog looking longingly for an invitation to go with its master. And then I imagined the change in demeanor when the invitation was issued. The dog didn't, in my imagination, hesitate to accept the invitation, and he was immediately ready for the adventure. I thought that, like most dogs, he started to wag his tail so hard that it looks like a tail wagging a dog.

I next considered how the dog would spring into action, jumping into the car next to his master. Everywhere they went his excitement would not be restrained, but bubbled over onto everyone coming near him.

When the dog was left alone, I thought of how he waited patiently for his master to return. He would rest; he would visit with passersby; and he would share his excitement with them. He wasn't idle.

This is also our story, isn't it, Father. Before someone issues the invitation to become Yours, there is a need for a life to change. I was so fortunate; my parents knew I would need the change so they prepared me for it. My parents took me to Your house from the beginning of my being to give me the opportunity to meet and to accept Jesus Christ and to start off on a new adventure—the adventure of a lifetime (again, an eternity to be exact).

As with the dog, my excitement shouldn't be restrained, but should be apparent to every passerby. He or she should be able to look at me and know that something is different about me—something has put a spring in my step. They should be able to talk with me and know that I have a joy in my heart to share. They should be able to listen to me, knowing that I am truly happy and believe with all my heart that what I know **is** real. These last three steps are witnessing, Father, witnessing for You. I am not to sit idly and watch the world go by without trying to make things better. As the dog did with the passersby, I am to be active and share with others.

Finally, Father, I mentioned the dog waiting for his master's return. I, too, wait for Christ's return. I am reminded to keep watch and to wait.

Father, please grant me the grace to share with everyone I can. As in the past, I know that when I do need to speak of You to someone, You are all sufficient and will help me as needed to get the task done. Thank You. You and Jesus Christ are good Masters. You are a great God, worthy of all adoration, praise, love and obedience.

I love You.

BYSTANDER OR PARTICIPANT

(7) "Beloved, let us love one another: for love is of God; and every one that loveth is born of God, and knoweth God. (8) He that loveth not knoweth not God; for God is love. (9) In this was manifested the love of God toward us, because that God sent his only begotten Son into the world, that we might live through him. (10) Herein is love, not that we loved God, but that he loved us, and sent his Son to be the propitiation for our sins. (11) Beloved, if God so loved us, we ought also to love one another." --1 John 4: 7-11

All good (and bad) things are known by You and all good things are from You. I can share my heart with You even though You already know what is in it. I know that when someone does something good for me, it is only appropriate to thank them. You, Father, are worthy of my thanksgiving, my sharing with You, my excitement in You, and of my praise.

This is Your day, Father—of course, every day is Your day, but this is "the Lord's Day." I speak so frequently about my pastor (thank You, again, for Pastor and his family—they are such blessings to me). Pastor spoke to us today from 1 John 4:7-11. He made a statement which caused me to ponder his example carefully; it made a lot of sense to me. He stated that in sports, if we are sitting on the sideline, it isn't as interesting as if we are involved in the game. Likewise, church is interesting, even exciting, if we get involved.

It doesn't really matter what we do in life, we are either a bystander or a participant. Again, it *is* always more interesting if we are involved. We can't personally affect change unless we become part of the solution through participation.

This basic thought of bystander vs. participant made me think of marriage. In marriage, we have individual accounts—much like bank accounts. He puts into his account and I put into my account. When we became married, You gave us a third account—a joint account, so to speak. We must both make deposits in that joint account, or we could find ourselves bystanders in our own marriage. As Pastor said, marriage isn't meant to be boring. It is meant to be exciting. It is to be a union of two people, not two people doing their own thing. This means, at times, putting some of my rights and expectations on hold. When I do this, everything received becomes a beautiful blessing from my spouse and from You.

I need to think about the other person on the account, my wonderful husband. Am I taking out more from the joint account than is my share? Do I meet that unexpected need of his and make sure I have made enough deposits of love, time, and attention to meet his needs? Am I within Your will in my marriage? Or, am I closing my eyes to fleeting opportunities to make deposits in our joint account?

Father, You know my husband and I don't agree on everything—few couples do. But, if we keep making deposits in our joint account, protected by the blood of Your Son, Jesus Christ, we will always have the security of a life together, available for eternity with You.

Thank You, Father, for our joint account. I pray that I increase my contribution to our life together by being faithful in love for him, obedient to You, and dedicated to his happiness in our time together on earth. I know that my happiness will be a reflection of his happiness. Again, my cup truly "runneth over." The 23rd Psalm assures me that: (Verse 6) *"Surely goodness and mercy shall follow me all the days of my life: and I will dwell in the house of the LORD for ever."*

This is also, in application, the promise of a home built on love, consideration, patience, and obedience to You. Thank You for Bill, Father. Grant me the grace to step outside of self and stand on the solid ground of a loving, caring, and sharing marriage.

I love You.

WINGS OF IRON OVER A SEA OF GLASS

Smooth sailing isn't guaranteed, but protection is.

Father, I am in the middle of a most wonderful trip, and it is time that I spend some quiet moments to share it with You and to thank You for my blessings. I have been waiting for months to go on this Alaska cruise with my loving extended family.

Each time I approach a ship for a cruise, I anticipate great things, and this trip was no exception. The beautiful ship carrying us is powerful and reliable enough to carry the vast weight of all passengers and crew, all of the baggage, and all equipment and supplies necessary for a safe voyage.

Even though we had never met the Captain and his crew, we put our trust in them—because they are in charge and they know what they are doing.

We departed from Seattle and headed for Alaska. Unlike taking the cruise from Anchorage south, we were on the open sea for the first two days and the sea was rough and unprotected. Many passengers were seasick and started looking for help. Once they found the doctor and followed his direction, things started to improve and soon we were in the Alaskan waters: smooth, beautiful and sheltered.

Once we reached the smooth Alaskan waters, we were blessed to watch one of Your majestic eagles soar across the heavens. All of this breathtaking, glorious beauty reminded me of You, Father. Everything was working together as You had planned it—unspoiled and perfect.

Cruising on the open sea reminded me of mankind, Your children, before we searched and found You. Life was not "smooth sailing": fear and danger existed in all directions. At times, we felt sick at heart or sick in attitude or just plain "sick and tired." We needed something. We searched and Christ's grace was shared with us. That is when we found You. Christ joined us for our cruise through life, and from that point on, carried and took care of all of our "baggage."

When we accept Christ as the Captain of our lives and we put our trust in Him, the seas of life calm, and we no longer need to fear the unknown storms coming in our direction—You, Christ, and the Holy Spirit are always there.

In considering the magnificent eagle, I am reminded of Psalm 91:4-5: *"He shall cover thee with his feathers, and under his wings shalt thou trust: his truth shall be thy shield and buckler. Thou shalt not be afraid for the terror by night; nor for the arrow that flieth by day."*

You will cover me with Your "feathers" of strength, and under Your "wings" I am safe and will live in trust. Your strength of iron can carry my every burden. Your beauty of life gives joy to my soul, and Your watchfulness as that of an eagle comforts me. I am shielded by truth—Your truth. Nothing can get to me through Your wings of iron, Father. You tell me: *"Because thou hast made the LORD, which is my refuge, even the most High, thy habitation; There shall no evil befall thee, neither shall any*

plague come nigh thy dwelling. For he shall give his angels charge over thee, to keep thee in all thy ways. They shall bear thee up in their hands, lest thou dash thy foot against a stone."
--Psalm 91:9-12

    As with my approaching a beautiful ship, each time I look up for You, I anticipate great things. I have only to keep looking up and You are there. When You hold me and shelter me in Your wings of iron, and as I abide in Your Word and trust in You, my journey in life is as smooth as this Alaskan sea of glass. Like a figurative sea of glass, I am fragile and at times feel breakable. And although trouble and trials may come my way, I trust they don't come to hurt me, but are for my eventual good. This is where trust and faith become two of my greatest blessings, Father. The help I **want** may not come immediately, but I am promised that it will come—at the right time: Your timing is perfect.

    I don't need to fear anything man, the world, or physical life can do to me. No angry wave can shake me out of Your grasp, dampen my delight in You, or send me into the depths. You **are** my rock and my salvation, my shelter in the time of storm, the One who told the sea, "Peace, be still," and it obeyed; the One who is faithful to His promises; the One whose mercies are everlasting; Thank You, Father. Thank You.

    I love You.

A MOUNTAIN RAILROAD

Don't let trash on the track set you back.

So much is on my heart at this time. This is a two-thought visit, Father. I would like to thank You for giving so many people the gift to write the beautiful songs of worship. I don't know the real name of this particular song, but I remember the message of the first line, "Life is like a mountain railroad." What a marvelous song, Father.

Hymns bring out emotions and truths which are hard to personally put into words, but You, through the inspired works of Your musicians, have given us this wonderful gift. "How Great Thou Art," "Amazing Grace," "It's Real," and "The Old Rugged Cross" are a few of my favorite worship and praise hymns. They bring praise to my mind and lips whenever I think of the words or when I sing them.

When I have a challenge or just need to be "picked up," one of my greatest blessings is when You give me a song in my heart. It runs through my mind day and night. I don't have time for whatever it is that is bothering me because my mind is full of You—the song does not come consciously, but miraculously. The next day I generally can't remember the song from the day before even though I sang through it or thought of the words at least fifty times. But, if I need it for a longer period of time, You let it linger until You have given me peace.

Many times, Father, as you know, when I have negative, not-so-sweet-spirited thoughts, I select a song appropriate to either open my heart to the Spirit or to lose my thoughts in You and Christ. I may not feel like singing, Father, but I know that it is what I need. It is true that if I apply the will to do something first, the emotion will follow. It is a simple thing that brings large results to a complex mind—sometimes even a child's chorus will speak volumes to me and reduces my tired adult mind to the simplicity of a child's understanding.

I think I'm finally getting to the second point of this talk with You, Father. We were on a trip when I saw a mountain railroad, and, of course, I thought of the old song and the truths it shares. This particular railroad was steep in many areas. I'm sure the engineer had to adjust his speed according to the environment: too much speed and he may not be able to avoid danger around the next curve. Too slow and he may not be able to keep up enough momentum to reach the heights.

Life, like a mountain road, has steep hills to climb; it contains unexpected dangers; it contains bumps along the way. I am figuratively told in this old song that I must be alert to dangers along the way of life and keep my "hands upon the throttle." I must adjust my speed in life to protect myself from the environment I find myself in. I am also told that I must keep my "eyes upon the rail." I must be vigilant; I must be conscious of everything around me in order to avoid dangers and temptations which come from all sides of life. I must keep my eye and mind on Christ, Your Will, and Your Word.

Thank You, Father, for bringing peace and joy to me through the ministry of Your musicians. Thank You for Your church where I learn and share the songs of worship with other Christians. Thank You, Father, for my "Blessed Redeemer," for Your "Unfailing Love," for Your "Pearly White City," and for Your "Amazing Grace."

I love You.

A FAITHFUL SOWER OF SEED

No seed, no harvest.

I was fondly thinking of one of my students and her daughter—Your daughters. Thank You for them, Father, they are very special to me. Thinking about them led me to thinking about my other students and how wonderful they were when I was in the classroom: what great joy they gave to me. They were, in my opinion the crème de la crème. They came to me from all backgrounds, all ages, all sizes, shapes, and colors; they were an amazing collection of potential. They were amazing, amazing, amazing!

My students were gifted, goal oriented, and dedicated; however, some never made it past the first month—they lost faith in their ability, gave up, lost sight of their goals, or let life interfere—opportunity lost, SEEDS FALLING UPON A ROCK.

Unlike those who quit, many expended effort equal to their goal and kept their heart and mind on their goal—not turning to the right or to the left, until all was completed. BUT, some students succeeded, only to, after a time, change directions in life because it wasn't what they expected it to be or because it was too demanding of their time. Similarly, a few succeeded and worked in their field, but health factors interfered and caused them to use their talents and gifts in other ways. They still applied what they knew, only within their physical abilities.

All had the same opportunity afforded them, but they were planted in different terrains of life. You know I love them, Father. I prayed for them daily on my way to work. They were all loved, just as a parent loves their children. However, there were those whose performance was below their potential and this brought sadness and disappointment—not in them, but in what they had lost. My heart ached for others in their trials and struggles. And then, they brought tremendous joy when they succeeded.

In this period of reminiscing, I was compelled to think of the parable of the seeds. Teaching has so many similarities to the spiritual application of Luke 8:5-15: *"A sower went out to sow his seed: and as he sowed, some fell by the way side; and it was trodden down, and the fowls of the air devoured it. And some fell upon a rock; and as soon as it was sprung up, it withered away, because it lacked moisture. And some fell among thorns; and the thorns sprang up with it, and choked it. And other fell on good ground, and sprang up, and bare fruit an hundredfold. And when he had said these things, he cried, He that hath ears to hear, let him hear. And his disciples asked him, saying, What might this parable be? And he said, Unto you it is given to know the mysteries of the kingdom of God: but to others in parables; that seeing they might not see, and hearing they might not understand. Now the parable is this: The seed is the word of God. Those by the way side are they that hear; then cometh the devil, and taketh away the word out of their hearts, lest they should believe and be saved. They on the rock are they, which, when they hear, receive the word with joy; and these have no root, which for a while believe, and in time of temptation fall away. And that which fell among thorns are they, which, when they have heard, go forth, and are choked with cares and riches and pleasures of this life, and bring no fruit to perfection. But that on the good ground are they, which in an honest and good heart, having heard the word, keep it, and bring forth fruit with patience."*

You tell my heart, Father, that all we can do *is* all that we can do. You gave us free choice. All we can do is teach, counsel, and advise our new Christian friends. The lesson of the seed is so real. We can't be one hundred percent successful. We can, on the other hand, be one hundred percent failure if we don't try to teach everyone we meet about You.

Teaching must be true—based on writings of the best authors we can find. You have written the text for me—Your Word. You, Father, are my master teacher. I pray I continue to be teachable until You take me Home. Father, please also present me with teachable students and let me plant the seed of Your Word—planted in the fertile soil of Your bountiful love. Please grant me the grace to tutor with love, understanding, and patience, but firm and unyielding in teaching what is right and true.

I love You.

FAITH, PRAISE, AND FAITHFULNESS

New life with Christ is like a big breath of fresh air—so breathe.

I'm feeling long-winded today, Father. We are so marvelously and wonderfully made.

We took a trip to Colorado last week. It was absolutely breathtaking—in more ways than one. The altitude at Pikes Peak made breathing very difficult for me, and I finally, consciously, thought about the blessing of the gift of every breath. I realize now how much I take for granted the wonderful blessing of breathing without difficulty. It seems as though I go through life without thinking about it and without giving You praise for it because You made my body so "user-friendly." It is just like the heart beating, the food digesting, sneezing, and who knows what else (other than You) I am receiving without showing proper appreciation. I sometimes think I pass through the wonderful miracle of life without thought about how truly marvelous it is.

The automatic reflexes of life are a lot like faith, Father. We breathe in the air and then we let "nature" take its course—it's automatic from that point forth. As Christians, we pray and then we can go on "cruise" emotionally, because we know Your Will, will be done. This is faith. Trust without worrying about it after it is once turned over to You.

Oh, why, Father, haven't I learned to faithfully thank You for what You have given me—**before** I ask for more? Why do I forget to thank You for the gift of another day, for the life of loved ones, for our spiritual leaders, for talents, and, yes, even for trials. In my trials, please help me to remember to thank You—anyway. We are told to give thanks in *all* things. Maybe this is so, at times such as these I can learn what I need to be taught and give You praise for every gift of life.

We must think about our prayers as the answers are received—whether the answer is "yes" or is "no," You are worthy of praise. Praise is a deserved response. It is a response from me to You for an expected or, in many cases, unspoken request that You have, in Your grace, granted me. Father, it must be a response from my heart and must be genuine and heartfelt or it is useless, shallow, dishonest flattery which is not pleasing to You.

When I have trials or challenges or tribulations or confusion or burdens or heartaches You never say to me, "take it easy, Joyce—relax"! Instead, You just tell me to have faith in You and to trust in You. You only ask that I turn it over to You and then You handle it the way it should be handled. I don't need to worry about it or worse yet, take it back and fret about it. I need to be persistent in my faith and remain faithful in my praising and petitioning—just as I know that the next breath will come without thinking about it because that is the way it is planned by You. *"Cast thy burden upon the LORD, and he shall sustain thee: he shall never suffer the righteous to be moved."* --Psalm 55:22

"Shall" is such a powerful word. From Your Word it assures me that You **will** sustain me. You don't tell me that You "might" sustain me—You **will** sustain me. That is a promise, the same as asking, seeking, and finding.

In 1 Peter 5:7 I am told: *"Casting all your care upon him; for he careth for you."*

Here, Father, I am told again to cast my cares upon You. Why? It is because of Your love for me. You would not deny me that which is right, pure, and in my best interest. Not that I deserve it or that it is what I want, but Your will is to give me what is best for me.

1 Peter 5:11 puts these other verses into perspective for me**.** *"To Him be all glory and dominion for ever and ever. Amen."*

I don't have a faith problem, Father. It is more of a "self" problem. I have faith to roll my burdens over to You, to forget them, to leave them at Your feet, to be faithful in praise and persistent in prayer. I have faith that You will lift me up and give me the counsel and calm I need to meet whatever the trial. I am just slow to turn it over to You—not because I don't trust You, but because I think it is very minor, and I should be able to handle it by myself. I will seek advice from others, but the one who knows the outcome of my every actions, I don't want to "bother." We have talked about this before, Father. Please forgive me for not getting over "self" and starting where I should start.

I need to start thinking of this as neglecting You by not relying on Your help from the very beginning. I know how I feel when I could help someone I love, but they don't want to "bother" me. We are working on this, though, aren't we, Father.

Father, please grant me the grace to persist in faith, praise, and faithfulness. Please don't let me give up; don't let me listen to the negativity of life; don't let me miss out on Your blessings because of my moments of weakness. And, Father, please don't let my action or lack of action block the Spirit's working in my Life. Father, I need Your strength as well as my faith in You to keep the small things from becoming insurmountable.

Thank You for such an easy way to visit with You. Please help me to rely on You first so I can see Your love for me and then witness of the same. I do trust You and have faith in Your marvelous power, mercy, love and promises. You are so excellent **all the time.**

I love You.

FRIENDS, FRIENDSHIP, AND FRATERNITY

Sharing with others is one of life's great joys.

Celebrating the station of friends as companions, friendships as a way of life, and fraternity as belonging to the human race, are worthy celebrations. Today two of my sisters in Christ (and partners in these letters), are meeting me for dinner in celebration of my birthday. Thank You for loving friends, Father. They add joy, comfort, a shade of silliness, and, of course, stability to our otherwise busy lives.

A friend can just say "Hi" to me and my burdens feel so much lighter and a smile extends from my heart to my lips. What a marvelous bodily function that is—a smile, I mean. The trick to the whole thing is that a smile isn't a natural reflex; it is a practiced response.

The joy of smiling carries, unfortunately, a serious side which is nothing to smile about. Some people have never had the environment afforded them to learn this beautiful gift we so take for granted. While visiting with You now, Father, I am so thankful for friends. I take friendship for granted because I have always been blessed with friends in my adult life. I firmly believe the old saying (paraphrased) "to have a friend one must, first, be a friend."

I have a burden for those who have never had friends because of circumstances in their past. They have never had anyone to trust, their trust has been broken, or they may even seem to be "invisible" to people around them. Many of them have never had friends from whom to learn.

My heart aches for the poor, the forgotten elderly, the sick, and the lonely. Many of these people have never been given a kind word, a friendly pat on the back, an understanding smile, or a loving helping hand. They are all Your children, Father. They need to know someone does care for them. Who better to care for them than another of Your children. We may seek the forgotten out, but we must remember that at times they need food for their stomachs before they can seek food for the soul. They will then sit to listen to the greatest love story of all time—the love of Jesus for them. How terrible it is to feel forgotten, unloved, unwanted—and yet, there are thousands of people like this in my own city.

It doesn't cost much or take much effort to send a smile to someone across the room. A little effort and time expended on a telephone call can yield priceless joy to someone needing caring contact. Minimal cost and a little effort can lead to a visit to someone who needs a touch of love in their life. A simple "How can I help You?" will generally open the door to someone's heart. Shaking the hand of a visitor at church and offering a seat, a Bible, or a songbook could make that person feel welcome and comfortable in Your house. It is amazing how little things such as these can produce large benefits to the giver as well as to the receiver.

A laugh from a person who has forgotten how to laugh is a beautiful thing. Some of the ways I can minister for You is through giving a financial boost to someone discouraged and struggling or providing a hot meal for someone hungry. I can give an evening of babysitting to a weary mother or be a volunteer who offers emotional, physical, or personal support for those in need. And, my personal favorite is to give a kind word or a hug **(if they hug)** to a senior saint. They've earned my respect. These are all worthy gifts—gifts of self—priceless gifts.

All of these acts require our conscious effort and a desire to live what we believe. You tell us that we will be blessed by being a blessing to others. We must keep things in perspective: first is You and Your Kingdom, second is our spouse and our vows, third is our family and then, others. By taking care of these responsibilities, we know we are furthering our first responsibility to You.

Father, please grant me the grace to be a friend. Help me be a friend to those who need a friend. Help me offer a kind word, a friendly hand, or even a helping hand. Let me make that friendly telephone call or a personal visit to someone You lead me to call or visit. Let me love others with Your love and give them the gift of two loving, caring friends—me and my Lord.

Thank You, Father, for friends who show me through their actions what friends are. Please bless them and this evening together. We know You will be there with us to celebrate my birthday.

I love You.

LITTLE IS MUCH

God inhabits our praise

I was talking to my friend (one of my "adopted" little sisters) yesterday, Father, and she, in passing conversation, used the words "It's a little thing that brings me joy." I pondered this profound statement—which gave me great joy—and thought of thirty things I receive regularly which bring me happiness, even great joy. I want to count a few praises for Your glory.

- Waking up in the morning after a good night's sleep
- Holding hands with Bill, a kind word, a loving touch
- A morning cup of coffee with Mom, Bill, and Max II
- A cool, gentle spring breeze
- Beautiful flowers—especially Your Pansy
- The first fruits of the season
- A cuddly kitten or puppy (especially Max II)
- A baby's or child's laughter, a loved one's laughter, and the laughter of a senior saint
- The voice of a friend
- A rainbow
- A sunrise or sunset
- A good sermon (thank You for Pastor)
- Reading Your Word
- Reading a good book (especially Dr. Charles Stanley)
- A good old hymn, an uplifting chorus, and "good" music
- A sweater on a cold day and a fuzzy blanket on a cold night
- Autumn colors, spring flowers, a gentle rain, and snowfall
- A happy memory crossing my heart
- Waterfalls, streams and canyons
- A visit or phone call from a friend

- Doing something "nice" for somebody else
- A walk in the park
- A ride in the mountains
- A loved one showing happiness
- Being around family
- Going to church and being around my church family
- Hummingbirds and other birds
- Watching squirrels and other critters
- And, oh, yes, chocolate

In my thought process, I thought about the times that these blessings crossed my path, but I didn't pay attention. I thought about Your Creation, how so many beautiful things can be lost in a fog, but once the fog lifts, the beauty is still there waiting for me to enjoy. You bless me that way, Father. If I miss a blessing the first time around, You still have it waiting for me when "the fog lifts." I particularly notice this in revisiting a sermon. When I revisit the notes from a sermon, I find that the Spirit is dealing with me presently in a completely different area of my life. I seem to notice something in the notes that did not get my attention the first time around. These are hidden blessings waiting for me to catch up—what a joy!

These things are all from You, Father: creation, love, nature, inspiration, and the senses of touch, sight, sound, and hearing. These are all constant sources of joy when our hearts are open to Your blessings.

I include my salvation at the top of *this* list of "free" sources of joy. Salvation is the highest blessing bestowed on us; it isn't a fleeting joy, but a joy which lasts for eternity.

Thank You for all the joys You bring to my heart on a daily basis. Father, it is true, the best things in life are free—gifts from You. I thank You for these blessings—seen or unseen. Thank You for bringing these joyful thoughts to my heart. Like the chorus says in part, little is **truly** much when You are in it.

I love You.

AS SOFT AS A LAMB'S EAR

Oh, that warm fuzzy feeling of gentle love.

Yesterday as I watered the flowers for Mom (Oh, Father, please protect Mom's flowers from me in her absence) and as I came to her little Lamb's Ear plant, I just had to share it with someone.

The Lambs Ear is a wonderful little plant: the leaves are about four to six inches long, oval in shape (tapering to a point at the end), silver green in color, and very soft and fuzzy—like a lamb's ear (but You know all of that). In addition to the leaf, the blossom of this plant is beautiful with its tall stem and its beautiful soft lavender shade. But, it's the softness and gentle touch of the leaf that fascinates and thrills me.

My sister-in-law, "Sister," from Colorado, is visiting, and I wanted to share this unique little plant with her, so I picked a leaf and brought it for her to see. She loved it as much as I do.

In considering this plant and the entire "episode" involved in sharing it, I thought of the leaf's gentle appearance and its softness. I also considered my picking it and how, after my picking it, it had to die—but it had to be picked in order for it to be shared.

This caused me to think of another Lamb, Father. Your Son Jesus Christ. This Lamb's ears always hear me when I "cry." He handles my troubles with a gentle touch. He, too, was sacrificed so that something good could be shared with others. I know this is totally a different situation, however, the leaf situation reminded me of the sacrifice of Christ on the cross: a sacrifice for me to share in truth with others.

I thought further that if I picked the leaf and did not share it and just let it die, it would have been sacrificed for nothing. (I know I'm making a mountain out of a mole hill here, Father, but I know You understand what I'm trying to say.) In this same thought pattern, if I know Christ died for me and do not share Him with others, I will not be giving Him His due praise. True, I would not have killed Him, and true, He would not have died in vain, but how unappreciative would I be? If a man or woman had saved my life while sacrificing his or her own, would I keep quiet about it? Would I be unappreciative? No! I would yell with the full force of my lungs how wonderful he or she was and what he or she did for me.

When it comes to Christ in all of His loving mercy, I, as a Christian, many times keep quiet when I should be shouting to the world about what He has done for me. Because of Him, I have forgiveness of sin—the sacrifice has already been made. I have eternal life—He made the way clear for me. I have the Holy Spirit—He sent a Comforter, guide, and counselor to me. He gently speaks to me through the Spirit telling me constantly that He loves me—He loved me enough to die for me.

Oh, thank You, Father, for Your beautiful flowers and the lessons they are able to teach me. Thank You for the Lamb's Ear which caused me to consider my gentle Savior. Thank You for Christ and His loving gift of grace—it is mine for the asking, mine for eternity. Thank You for the daily assurance through Your Word that You gave me Your Son so that through Him I might have life and have it more abundantly with You.

I pray that I do not, in my forgetfulness, get sidetracked from giving praise where praise is due, and do not let Jesus' sacrifice be made without sharing with everyone about it and sharing this gift of a new life given to me from the last, perfect, and purest sacrificial Lamb.

I love You.

COME AND DINE

Spiritual growth comes from spiritual foods.

What a wonderful old chorus, Father, "Come and Dine." It is such a wonderful inspiration. This song reminds me of a scene we came across on I-5 on a trip to Oregon. We saw a large field full of animals: some resting, some grazing, some wandering around, and some just standing, "surveying their kingdom." There was another group of animals under a large, elongated, open shed. Some of those were eating what had been prepared for them while others were resting. It was a pastoral scene—heartwarming.

In considering this picture, I was led to ponder how it came about and what purpose it was serving (I love thinking about such things). It was obvious that some animals were eating and that others were just resting out of the heat. Others came to the shelter at a later time to feed. I imagined the owner drawing out, according to his purpose, the plan for the feeding shed. I then imagined his sons building the shed according to their father's instructions from the plans that he shared with them. This shed not only provides a place of shelter for the rancher's animals, but, within the shed, the food also was protected from the storms. This whole scene and my resulting thoughts left me with a feeling of peace and serenity: it was so undisturbed, beautiful and natural.

This feeling led me to think of You and Your Word. We are all part of Your many creations: each with different needs and with different life's schedules. One thing we have in common is the need to be fed. Some come to the "table" later than others, but the table is always set, waiting for all who will come.

At the beginning of time, Father, You made a plan. Mankind was included in that plan, but many times strayed, so You drew out Your plan to feed the hunger of all who would partake: a permanent feeding location containing everything necessary for our survival. You gave this plan to Your selected children to build. The results: Your inspired Word, the Holy Bible, filled with food for growth, food for the soul, and food for thought. What a feast You provided for us.

Focusing on the shed that was sheltering the food shifted my thoughts and reminded me of our (meaning Christians) responsibility to keep Your Word undisturbed, unaltered, and unpolluted. You tell us in the Bible that You will always preserve Your Word, but there are those who have tried to alter it, and those unknowingly eating from another table may be left with an anemic soul. We *are* responsible for keeping our own dining room clean, aren't we, Father? We must shelter the food of Your Word.

Another thing impresses me about the feeding, Father. The shed and food are always available, like salvation; however, the hungry must come under the protection of the shed, Your protection, to get the food. One can have a Bible, but the food provided for us is under the cover. We must open it to read and receive the full value from it. Once we accept Christ into our hearts through salvation, the Holy Spirit is there to help us understand what we need to "digest" for our spiritual growth.

We are welcome to partake of Your meal, Father, but when we become Your child, Your Word is always easy to find, the pages are always full—all we need to do is look under the cover and partake of the contents. The "food" inside is given to everyone, so all have the opportunity to receive a complete diet of spiritual and emotional "vitamins." For Christians, if taken daily it will lead to a healthy daily existence and a soul which will last for eternity with You and Your Son, Jesus Christ.

Thank You, Father, for Your plan, for the feeding of Your children, for Your selected children who put Your plan into the inspired pages of Your Word, for Your shepherds who show us where to find the "food," and for Your invitation to come and dine at Jesus' table. You are an awesome God, a good God, and a great God.

I love You.

THE REAL DEAL

A "real deal" will live and grow and multiply.

I was sitting in a business the other day, Father. There wasn't anything particularly special about it, but there **was** this large artificial plant in the corner of the room. I started to think about the concept of artificial "this, that, and the other thing."

An artificial plant is wonderful for atmosphere and colorful touches around the house or around a business, but they are generally only for that and for casual observation—nothing lasting or uplifting. They take very little care—but the texture is artificial and the aroma is artificial or, in most cases, nonexistent. They never grow or produce flowers from a bud.

I find that with the artificial plants I have at home, I put them in place, think "that is a nice touch," and from that time on I give them an occasional glance, but I receive no real inspiration from them.

As I sat looking at the artificial plant, (I was gratified it was there—it **was** a nice touch) I began to think more deeply about artificial versus the real deal. The looks are close; however, the artificial plant is expendable. It gathers dust and gets either cleaned up or thrown away by its owner. Ouch!

I then thought about genuine versus artificial "Christians." Real Christians are like living plants. They call me to take a closer look and to breathe in the living fragrance of their love. They touch me with their softness and leave me wanting more. When they are gone, I miss them and look for more with the same beauty to continue their purpose in my life. Real Christians live and breathe Your Word, Father. If fed, they multiply in number and provide beauty in life. In addition to this, the joy of the Spirit gives them beauty beyond the beauty of a wonderful flower. The touch of a real flower is soft and alive just as the forgiving gentle words of a Christian touching the heart.

The smell of a real flower draws a person to partake of its gift. Living, breathing, forgiving Christians also draw others to themselves and eventually to You—artificial won't work here, Father, even though You can use anything or anyone to accomplish Your purpose.

A real flower attracts attention time and time again. I return to drink in its beauty, to touch it, to admire it and to receive comfort from its life. Flowers lighten a burden and draw praise from my lips to my Creator, my God, and my Redeemer. Like being drawn to this real flower, I am drawn to Your children, Father. The comfort and joy I receive from them come directly from the source—You. There is nothing artificial about it; it is the real deal.

Father, I want to be real, genuine, and available. I want to "walk the walk" and not just "talk the talk." As the old saying goes, "Talk is cheap." The price Christ paid for my birthright and for my forgiveness was too high for cheap talk.

Father, grant me the grace to live and breathe Your Word, to exercise Your gentle response, to display Your mercy, and to offer forgiveness without hesitation. And, Father, please grant me the blessing of returning again and again to my garden of Godly friends where we are faithfully fed Your formula for our Christian growth.

Above all, Father, let me be genuine in my thoughts, deeds, and prayers. You are the source of my strength. Let my roots stay deeply grounded in Your Word and help me "bloom where I am planted." Then, when the blossom is finished, I will know that I have served my purpose. Thank You, Father, for these thoughts.

I love You.

A VIEW FROM THE TOP

The clouds will pass and things will appear clear again. Take heart.

    Father, I was thinking about our family trip of a few weeks ago. We spent a wonderful day in Seattle at the Space Needle.

    The Space Needle stands so tall—as though reaching for the sky. The trip from the ground level to the top was smooth and F-A-S-T. Once on the top level, the scenery was spectacular: no traffic to avoid, no rushing, no busy people, and no obstructions of my view. Things looked smaller when I looked down at the city, and of course, the restaurant at the top of the tower revolved so absolutely nothing was missed. Everything was seen, one section at a time.

    As time passed, however, the clouds covered the entire city and visibility was only in select areas. Why is it that so many things in life keep me from seeing clearly: daily rushing, stresses, responsibilities, social activities, relationships, habits, and anything else in life which clouds my growth? In asking this question, a thought came to mind: I am looking at all of these from the ground level. When I look at them and they become clouded, I should look at select areas which can be seen clearly. I should look at them from the highest height—through Your Word as seen through Your eyes, Father. When I defer to Your view of my life through Your Word, and the simplicity of revolving my view around You, life's trials look smaller and the whole portrait of my being is a much larger and brighter picture. The joy of the Spirit pushes the clouds away, making a clear path from my heart to You.

I know, Father, that everything in this life will not be perfect, but "everything will be all right"—unimaginably great for eternity. You promised, and You are faithful to Your Word. Thank You for Your unlimited goodness.

Father, please grant me the grace to wait in patience, to look heaven-ward with anticipation for Your good, and to marvel at Your glory and mercy. Grant me the grace to stand tall in my faith and reach out to You when I'm not seeing my daily path clearly. Please grant me the grace to study and listen, pray and listen, and learn and act. I know that if I want a Godly view, I need to seek the view from the top—the view through Your eyes.

I love You.

LIFE IS LIKE A PEANUT BUTTER CRACKER

It "ain't" all bad.

Good morning, Father. This is such a beautiful day. Thank You for the gifts of a restful night, for Your beautiful morning, for Your love, and for Your faithfulness to Your promises. I pray that my heart, my mind, and my lips are pleasing to you on this gift of another day, and I pray that the choices I make today will glorify You.

This morning I am thinking about peanut butter crackers. It's a highly unlikely subject for praise, Father. I don't particularly know why I'm thinking about them, possibly because I haven't eaten breakfast yet, and I'm a little hungry.

A package of peanut butter crackers is such a small thing, but it can give so much enjoyment when shared with the right company. Mom and I love peanut butter crackers. They are wonderful—***until*** someone puts the cracker down on a damp napkin and the bottom gets a little soggy. But of course, this doesn't slow me down because the top is still crispy and the inside is still wonderful.

Life is a lot like this, isn't it, Father? It is somewhat like a peanut butter cracker with a soggy crust and a crispy crust. (You know I don't mean that literally.) What I mean is that life is sandwiched in between good choices and bad choices—just like the good (crispy) cracker and the bad (soggy) cracker. As with the whole "cracker," it doesn't have to be thrown away or wasted for the ingredients to remain pleasing. All we have to do is just remove or correct the bad layer. It has only suffered a temporary "infirmity."

Praise You, Father, that You don't throw us away because we, at times, have developed ugly spots from making poor choices. You have Your Spirit available to convict us and lead us to Your Word so that the bad layer can be removed or corrected. And You help us clean up the mess we have made.

If we ask for forgiveness, we have only to go to Your Son, Jesus Christ, to forgive us for the poor choices we make in life. We know, with Your loving care, that this period of weakness shall also pass.

I praise You for the promise of entering into Your presence—PERFECT. What an encouragement. I guess I need to do a little more practicing doing things Your way, though. Teach me Your Word, Father; give me the strength of character to strive with all my heart to please You with every thought, word, and action. Although I have my "not-so-good" side, Father, please use my heart which is filled with the Holy Spirit and let me keep my good side "whole" for Your work.

I love You.

WHAT'S UNDER THE COVER?

Let my life reflect Christ's likeness

Good morning, Father. Thank You for another lovely, sunshiny day.

I was sitting in another waiting room the other day; so, I pondered, as usual, thinking of You. This time I was sitting close to a magazine rack so I looked at the visible covers to see what was available. Some of them I am familiar with, others are unfamiliar. There were magazines on travel, food, and fashion (some good and some far away from my likes or understanding—I'm trying to be kind here, Father).

After looking at the front row of covers, I got up to look at the rest of the selection. I found a great variety of materials. Some were acceptable for believers. Others were okay, but not likely to be very beneficial. Some were helpful, others detrimental; some informative, some were "brain drain." Some portrayed a beautiful picture of life, and others portrayed only the ugly side of life.

In reality, whether we want to believe it or not, most of us can be read like a magazine. We may have a beautiful cover, but the contents may need revision or, in the least, editing. We think we are hiding that "garbage" under the cover; however, garbage has a way of smelling up the whole area so that it can always be found.

What areas of my life need editing today, Father? thoughts? action? lack of action? words? These are all eventually visible areas once the cover is lifted.

Are my actions, words, or thoughts helpful or are they detrimental? Am I, or others, learning from them or are they just "brain drain" and wasted time? Are they, when needed, sanctioned by Your Word or are they just from my limited power? Do I, Father, portray, inside and outside of my being, a beautiful view of life or show others a confusing, misleading view of a Christian's life? These are some other things You have placed on my heart to ponder.

Praise You, Father, that You see right though the cover, directly to the areas which need to be cleaned up. Father, please continue to edit my life with the red marks: the red blood that Christ shed for the cleansing and remission of my sin. The red which can continue to wash away the detrimental sins I gather up along life's way. Thank You, Father, for sending Your Son who covers me with His grace. Father, when people read me like a magazine, please grant me the grace to have them see Your Word in action—from cover to cover.

I love You.

THERE'S A ROCKY ROAD AHEAD—MAYBE.

Oh, Lord, I yearn for the day my road is even and my bumps smoothed out.

Construction, construction, construction! Sometimes I think there is nothing going on here, but construction. It's hard, Father, to sit in the car waiting for a construction crew member to wave me through.

"Wait a minute, Joyce! *They* are the ones in the heat of the day, fixing something you have been complaining about for months, looking at the frowns on the faces in each car, and then going home completely drained of their strength."

Oh, Oh. Is that what You are telling my heart, Father? Oops! Sorry, Father. I guess I was thinking of ME again. How often I do that. Forgive me for this, Father. I need to work more on getting over "self."

I was thinking about how unwanted this basic situation is. But it is also a matter of great need and, as so, is also wanted. It is a matter of attitude. I guess I can sit here and grumble to myself, or I can look beyond myself and be pleasant. Again, Father, it is a matter of attitude—good or bad. What will it be? What will *I* do? Will *I* make everyone around me miserable? Will I join the "pity party"? I really don't want people to guess whether I am Yours or not, Father. I want them to know beyond a shadow of a doubt that I am Your child. Am I going to be a smooth surface or a bumpy road which needs resurfacing? I need to keep that question constantly on my mind and think about it before I respond to others, or in many cases, react instead of respond.

There are many things I can do while I wait—all very enjoyable. I can listen to music. I have some wonderful music tapes—uplifting and inspirational. I can listen to one of Pastor's sermons (thank You again, Father, for Pastor and his family). I can sing hymns (praise You, Father, that You judge my heart and not my voice). I can pray without ceasing as You have instructed me in Your Word. And, my favorite, I could praise You. I could just look out the window and start praising. I could praise You for the men and women who are working to improve things for my life. There are things around me which are beautiful and praiseworthy. There is the night's rest that I received that I can praise You for. (If I neglected to thank You for that earlier in the day). I could praise You for the beautiful day You have given me (no matter the weather because You are there and You have wonders waiting for me).

With You, every day is a beautiful day, Father. I have hope; I have answered prayer; I have family and friends; I have Your church and church family; I have my mind and physical capabilities; and I always have You to talk with. Thank You for keeping me under construction. I don't like the bumps I put in my life's road and You have a miraculous way of straightening me up and leveling me out.

I love You.

LET THE SON SHINE IN—AND OUT

Well, button my lip.

My thought today, Father, is not a pleasant one for me to talk about, but all Christians must face it from one side of the fence or the other.

I don't know why I thought of this subject because it all started out with something beautiful. The clouds were beautiful today, Father. They were so light and fluffy. The beauty today was in their softness and in their airy appearance. In thinking more about clouds, I also thought of the heavy ones which hide the sun. They shade the earth from the hot sun, but are not cheerful.

I then considered the dark, stormy clouds. These clouds are fast moving, collecting other storm clouds along the way, and, pretty soon, fill the whole sky so I can't see the sun at all. These storm clouds tell me that there is a storm forming: lightning could strike at any moment. Floods could be in the future, and things could become very dangerous.

Then, there is fog, Father. A fog can keep me from seeing clearly. It is a sweeping mist which can encircle me and keep me from proceeding to my destination.

Gossip is a lot like this, Father. It starts out as a light cloud of information floating from one person to another. People become lost in the fog of confusion. Gossip is one of the most destructive weapons in the human arsenal. It has no purpose.

It starts because someone knows something that someone else doesn't know (and doesn't need to know) and shares it without thought. It continues gaining size and momentum (like the building up of clouds) It may start out as light conversation, but soon becomes the main topic of discussion, mulled over in the mind, and then "billows" on.

Gossip should never be shared in the first place. This person who is hurt in the process may never seek confidence again from a brother or sister in the church. Oh, Father, too many of Your children who were seeking help have left their church because of a "harmless" conversation with a friend.

The subsequent conversations participated in by some of those hearing the original "story" are not so harmless. The story develops into a thickened cloud of fact. At worst, the purpose of passing it on is just to make one story "better" than the last one. At best, it could be because some facts have been forgotten, have become embellished with half truths and were added without thought.

By the time the gossip has circulated a few times, it turns into a heavy, thick cloud of confusion and pain. The friendly church is no longer a friendly church to the person who is the subject of the gossip. Oh, Father, this is so in opposition to what You want from Your children and Your church.

By the time the situation is finished, the clouds of gossip become dark and stormy. They do have danger wrapped up in them. A person can come to the Lord by Your power and our efforts, but can be "destroyed" by careless words or demeanor: the person seeking help in the beginning can now become lost in an all-encircling fog of confusion about what the Christian life is all about. They no longer see Christ, but see the gossiping Christian as representative of Christian beliefs. They start reading people instead of Your Word. They start missing more church and they stop seeking help and fall back into what is "comfortable."

There is no such thing as friendly gossip, Father. It is conflicting in terms and contrary to Your teachings. To take, in application, something my pastor said a long time ago (Thank You, again, Father, for my pastor and family). In essence, he said: I do not need to see the dirty laundry of a fellow Christian in order to help fix the washing machine.

Father, grant me the grace to be a true friend: one who listens and prays. Please convict me to keep my heart open, my mind on prayer and praise, and my mouth shut in confidence.

Please, don't let me *start*, *pass on*, or *listen* to gossip. Father, help me to accept people, in Your love, even though the actions may be something of which I do not approve.

Please let Your Son shine in my heart; help me seek the Spirit's counsel for whatever help I am allowed to offer and for the strength to stay within my "place" according to Scripture. Help me to be a trusted member of my friendly church, to open up my heart, and let Your Son shine out.

I love You.

A SECOND LOOK AT LIGHT, FLUFFY CLOUDS

Your Glory in the beauty of the heavens.

Father, The other day in "Let The Son Shine In—And Out" I talked with You about clouds. It was totally away from my purposed talk of praise with You. I seemed to have gone way beyond the light, fluffy clouds directly to the dark, stormy ones. I feel, however, that I needed to discuss this human flaw with You to bring it afresh to my own mind and heart. I don't want to fall into the gossip trap.

Today, Father, I'm not going beyond the light, fluffy clouds unless You want me to go farther.

Thank You, Father, for Your fluffy clouds. They are so beautiful against the cheerful blue sky. As the large rocks add aesthetic dimension to Your coastline, Your clouds equally add visual depth and beauty to the heavens above.

In Your Word, You speak to us of clouds in many different ways:

- ***A Symbolic Reference:*** Hosea 6:4: *"O Ephraim, what shall I do unto thee? O Judah, what shall I do unto thee? for your goodness is as a morning cloud, and as the early dew it goeth away."*
- ***A Revelation Reference:*** Revelation 14:14: *"And I looked, and behold a white cloud, and upon the cloud one sat like unto the Son of man, having on his head a golden crown, and in his hand a sharp sickle."*
- ***A Pillar:*** Exodus 16:10: *"And it came to pass, as Aaron spake unto the whole congregation of the children of Israel, that they looked toward the wilderness, and, behold, the glory of the LORD appeared in the cloud."*
- ***A Protector:*** Matthew 17:5: *"While he yet spake, behold, a bright cloud overshadowed them: and*

behold a voice out of the cloud, which said, This is my beloved Son, in whom I am well pleased; hear ye him." **(This reference to the cloud is repeated again in Luke 9: 34-35.)** *"You protect us from the glory of Your presence, for we are not yet physically, mentally, or emotionally ready to witness it. It is so much more than we could humanly imagine."*

All of these, coming together, add up to a large, billowing cloud of blessing and promise. Not a dangerous storm cloud or a frightening dark mass, but a large, beautiful reminder of You.

Thank You for Your beauty. Thank You for Your promises. Thank You for Your loving kindness and grace. Thank You for giving me Your wonderful Son and Spirit so my life will be soft, Godly, and heaven-bound.

I love You.

MIRROR, MIRROR ON THE WALL

God's gift to me is the mirror of His Word.

What a "trip" it is to look in the mirror when I'm getting dressed to go out. I never know where this trip will take me—it could take me to the closet multiple times. The good thing about looking in the mirror is that it gives me a second chance. I look in it, survey what I see, and it can give me a second chance to get it right—whatever "it" is.

A second chance in getting ready to go somewhere is a good thing. It can lead to positive change—*if* my purpose is to look better. The trip to the mirror may lead to some required changes and it may take multiple attempts to become what I want others to see. If I like what I see, I keep it. If I don't like what I see, I keep on changing until it is right.

One thing about looking in a mirror is that it should be a clear mirror, not a clouded mirror. A clouded mirror gives an unclear view. A cracked mirror is even worse, because it give a distorted view: sort of half right and half wrong.

You have given me a mirror to life, Father: Your Word. It shows me what things I am doing right; it shows me what needs to be changed; and it lets me know how to make the changes. It lets me see behind me—my past as an unredeemed sinner and my past as a redeemed child. Your Word goes even further, Father, and shows me my future.

Thank You, Father, for Your Word and for the reflection of what I should look like—all the time, not just when I go out. Thank You for letting me see the future through Your promises. I pray that I always try to do the best I can for You: that I look in Your mirror of life and make the necessary changes or corrections.

At times I can't see flaws in my makeup. It is at these times that I rely on others close to me to **gently** point out what needs to be taken care of. I pray that my Godly friends let me know when changes need to be made, things that I could not see.

    I believe in answered prayer, Father. I know that I will be able to step out, clothed in faith and clothed in Your forgiveness, everlasting mercy, and grace. Let me be a mirror for You, Father, reflecting these treasured images of Your love on to everyone I meet, knowing that what they see is true. It may not be fashionable by today's standards, but it is right. Thank You.

    I love You.

SECOND-HAND BLESSINGS

When the Holy Spirit prompts, do it and enjoy a joy shared.

  The telephone rang this evening. The time was a little late, but not really too late for a friendly call. As You already know, Father, it was a friend calling to see if it was early enough, or too late, to wish Mom a happy 90th birthday. Wow! That's a real friend! Of course, it wasn't too late, so I joyfully took the telephone to Mom.

  Mom was so encouraged and happy to know that someone cared and called to wish her a happy birthday. She smiled a lot and shared a brief conversation with our friend—the smile lasted much longer than the phone call. Mom's face muscles probably got tired of smiling, but her heart, I'm sure, was still grinning from chamber to chamber. (That's another amazing bodily function.)

  Terry called to be a blessing to Mom (that, she did) But, it went further than that. You see, Father, I found myself smiling, also, and my heart continued to be light all evening just to see Mom happy and to know that someone showed a kindness to one of my loved ones.

  I thought about my childhood years—during "the war"—when most of the things we had were either homemade or second-hand. I thought how, Father, what really happened this evening was, Terry sent a blessing to Mom, but I received the "second-hand" blessing—the blessing that was originally intended for someone else, but a portion of the blessing ended up hanging on my heartstring. I treasure this as much as I do my old hand-me-down Bible.

  This caused me to think: You tell me in Your Word that any grace or peace I show to others will not be given in vain. However, You also tell me that I am to give for Your honor and glory—not for reward or expectation of a reward. *"I have shewed you all things, how that so labouring ye ought to support the weak, and to remember the words of the Lord*

Jesus, how he said, It is more blessed to give than to receive."
--Acts 20:35

This passage speaks of giving of my resources, but it also tells me I am blessed when I am a blessing to others. When I receive a blessing, there is no doubt who is sending it my way. It is generally through someone else, but is sent from You—and Your timing, as always, is perfect.

In considering second-hand blessings, something else comes to mind, Father: another wonderful thing about second-hand *this or that* is that it is actually the "real thing"—it is just received a little later than the original. Additionally, in order for an item to go from one person to another person (and yes, even another or another or another) it must be of great quality—something which will endure. Anything done for others to Your glory is of the best quality, whether large or small. I am reminded, again, of Mrs. F. W. Suffield's song, "Little is Much, When God is in it." Oh, praise You, Father, how true that is.

When I am a blessing to others and I "feel good" about it, I receive that blessing from You. I know when I am blessed because my heart lets me know. I am blessed; the receiver is blessed, and You are glorified. As Your musician George Schuler wrote, Father, and I pray ". . .make me a blessing to someone today."

I love You.

SHOWERS OF BLESSINGS

Like the rain, God's blessings just keep coming.

I'm still being blessed by yesterday's thoughts, Father. I want to share the story of another blessing with You. You already know about it, but I'm sure You wouldn't deny me the blessing of tracking them. There are a lot of "blessings" included with the giving of just one gift of self, aren't there, Father?

Blessing Numbers 1-2 (+): One of Your couples, Jessica and Patrick, gave us a delightful Christmas gift. (Each received the blessing of **giving**—possibly multiple blessings as they thought of each gift and receivers of their many gifts.)

Blessing Numbers 3-5: Mom, Bill, and I received the gift: the blessing of **receiving**.

Blessing Numbers 6-7: The gift was hand-made, so Mom and I knew that a lot of love was put into it. We received the blessing of a gift of **love**.

Blessing Numbers 8-10(+): The three of us enjoyed eating the gift from our friends and appreciated their thoughtfulness—*each time* we returned to the table. They gave us the blessing of **enjoyment**.

Blessing Number 11: Mom thanked them by sending a note, allowing Mom to experience the blessing a second time in thought. She received the blessing of showing **gratitude**.

Blessing Numbers 12-14: I was blessed to deliver the note to Jessica; she was blessed by knowing that the gift was appreciated and that their gift was enjoyed. If the note was shared with Patrick, as I'm sure it was, than he also received a blessing. We were able to share the blessing of **friendship**.

Blessing Number 15: I was blessed to see Jessica so happy and to hear her laugh. I received the blessing of **joy.**

Blessing Number 16: Another of Your children, witnessed Jessica's delight and, in turn, smiled and showed happiness.

She received the blessing of shared **happiness, friendship, and inclusion**.

Blessing Numbers 17-22: Today, we shared the "goodies" with three guests who thoroughly enjoyed them and appropriately thought it was "fabulous." This was the blessing of **sharing** for us **and** the blessing of **receiving** for them.

I know I have probably missed listing many blessings shared, but this is okay, it is just a quick look at one incident which brought a lesson to my heart.

Well, Father, that just about covers my thoughts, however, I have "banked" some blessings for Sunday. On Sunday, I will tell Jessica and Patrick how much our guests enjoyed their thoughtfulness. They will be blessed; I will be blessed, and again, You will be glorified by our actions. That's a whole shower of blessings that Jessica and Patrick mixed up for Your glory, Father. And, I imagine that when they read this—which they will—they will, again, be blessed. What they thought was just a simple gift turned out to be a 22-hand-plus blessing,—ALL FROM ONE WONDERFUL ACT OF THOUGHTFULNESS AND LOVE. Father, please grant me the grace to see the wonderful variety of blessings I receive on a daily basis.

Father, You created blessings. Everything we have, are, or will become, is from You. Our biggest blessings which can never be duplicated is Your love for us by giving us life and for sending us Your Son, Jesus Christ. Our biggest blessing from Christ is the giving of His life for our eternal salvation. These gifts cannot be equaled. We can, however, be faithful in creating a silent thunder which announces the shower of blessings through helping, sharing, giving, and loving.

I love You.

PILLOWS OF CLOUDS

"The heavens declare the Glory of God. . . ." --Psalm 19:1

It is just a time of praise and conversation, again, Father. We took a wonderful trip to Oregon, but the weather was a little unpredictable. The sky was filled with dark clouds and the promise of rain to come. We received Your blessing of a little rain, but I noticed that once the rain stopped, soft pillows of clouds started separating from the larger bodies of darkness, playing a graceful prelude to the sunshine.

As the clouds increased in number and rhythm, I thought of them as a visual testimony of Your goodness, grace, and promise sweeping across the world, going from one person to another to another. Not literally, as You know, Father, but accepting it as one of the many reminders of Your power. It is only appropriate that this scene lead me to think of You. You are the Creator of everything, and everything is a result of Your creation and power. Why shouldn't I be able to see You and Your power in **every** good thing—if I seek it?

You created my heart, my mind and my lips. Similar to the visual stimulation of Your clouds, my heart, mind, or lips can generate either "storm clouds" of ungodly behavior, or "soft, refreshing clouds" of goodness and Godliness. When someone observes me—my actions and words—do they see You in me? I pray they do, Father.

Storm conditions of ungodly "behavior" can be manifest in harmful, hurtful, or hateful thoughts or words. Oh, Father, help me; guard my heart, mind, and lips from darkness and guide me consciously to the softer delights and examples of Your holiness and love. Father, please fill me with Your Sweet Spirit to share Your unconditional, incredible, awesome love with others. Lord, please make me a blessing and a good example. Graciously let Your love pass from my heart, mind and lips to those I float by in life. Let me be a welcomed introduction to Your Kingdom, not a dark cloud of indifference and disappointment.

I love You.

IT'S WHAT'S UNDERNEATH
THAT COUNTS

Beware of those deep, hidden "life wreckers."

I was looking at a picture from an Alaska cruise, Father, specifically a picture of a large calving glacier. This is a breathtaking, exciting experience.

It all starts with a startling **Crack**! This "crack" is followed by tons of ice sliding or falling into the water below, causing a tremendous splash—rocking any boat or ship in its wake. After the breaking off of the ice, smaller bergs churn and turn in the water until they gain their center of gravity and eventually settle. This process initially stirs up a lot of impurities, but soon the impurities disappear and the water is, once again, smooth and clear. Once settled, an extremely large percentage of the iceberg rests below the surface of the water, giving it stability.

This memory held two lessons for me. The first is that You use me, Your child, to create the right conditions for a new Christian to settle into his or her new life as Your new child. New and old Christians can be, figuratively speaking, compared to a calving glacier: the glacier being a mature Christian and the calved iceberg, a new Christian setting out in a new life. Once we have mentored a new Christian he or she needs to break away and settle in Your Word. You have provided the living waters. There will be churning and turning until the new Christian has settled with You as his or her strength and balance. Once the person finds Christ, he or she will finally find rest in life—impurities washed away, churnings controlled, and permanently immersed in the cleansing waters to stay pure.

The second lesson that this scene brought to mind, Father, is that beauty is only skin deep. I was taught this by my family, and I hear people say this time and time again. When I look only to the surface of someone or something, it is the same as boating in waters of icebergs and not paying attention to what is underneath the surface of the water. It *is* what's underneath that does count.

If I don't look deeply enough or if I ignore the depth, I could miss the important, big picture. And, like the iceberg and the ship, collide and destroy what utility I could have been for You. The real problem here, Father, is that instead of a ship wrecking, it's a soul that may crash and burn. I may never have a second opportunity with that person.

When I am obedient, I create favorable conditions on the growth of my witnessing. Like the iceberg, I do need favorable conditions for growth. It is much like what I can do on my own versus what I can do with You: what I can do on my own is similar to the tip of the iceberg: a small part of the whole. But, with Your help, Father, immersed in faith, I **can** do all things through Christ. I have a never ending source of strength as long as I rely on the greater strength, YOU, to give balance in my witnessing. Grant me the grace to find my balance in my Savior, Christ Jesus.

I love You.

WHEN IS A LEAF NOT A LEAF

*Nature will, many times, tell you about its Creator.
Look for its message.*

Father, what a wonderful thought I had today because of one of Your beautiful flowers, a Calathea. I was admiring its beautiful leaf and noticed that it was an enormous leaf with the impression of a second leaf which, again, held the impression of a third leaf. What a unique concept: three in one. I decided to call it my trinity plant—actually Mom's trinity plant. Every time I look at it, it will bring to mind the most wonderful trinity of life: You, God the Father, Christ, God the Son, and my Comforter, God the Holy Spirit.

The outer level of the leaf reminded me of You, Father. It is strength, beauty, and the life blood of everything it holds. It is the basis of this beautiful trinity: holding everything else within its framework.

The second impression of a leaf is bolder; however, the outline color of this impression is melted into the color of the first, making it a perfect blend and showing that it is a part of the whole. The boldness shows that it is special; the focal point of the whole plant. This reminded me of Your precious Son, Jesus Christ.

Each leaf has many sections resembling brush strokes. The third impression of a leaf, the inner impression, is at the heart of the leaf. It is a whisper: light, refreshing, pure, and coming, appropriately, *after* the second. Each outgrowth of this impression gently brushes corresponding sections of the other two "leaves" weaving them into a solid unity. This is much like the working of the Holy Spirit, tying our lives in conformity to that of the example set by Christ and to Your Will for us.

One other thought which blessed me today, Father, is that the back of this entire leaf is blood red. How appropriate, because our salvation is secured by the Blood of Christ. It is the backing and basis of our faith and for all of our beliefs.

Father, I thank You for a totally delightful thought this day. When is a leaf not a leaf? It ceases being a leaf when it has a lesson to teach. It then becomes a personal message from You which is a much higher calling.

I love You.

CAN YOU HEAR ME NOW?

People are listening. Is it worth hearing?

Some of our teens sang the special for our Wednesday evening service. Our children and youth are such blessings to me. Thank You, Father, for our wonderful, service-to-Christ oriented young people. Please grant me the grace to let them know that they have blessed me and continue to bless me from week to week.

I noticed the microphones in place on the stage. The microphones were on stands, but the girls picked them up and took control of the delivery. The song was wonderful in words, spirit, and voice.

Singing in front of a group of people is difficult enough, but a microphone can be paralyzing. In looking back at this experience, I thought of how much life without Christ is like microphones on stands. Life is intimidating. What if I make a mistake? Everyone will hear the mistake. What if I don't use the tool given to me, the microphone; will I be heard at all?

If a microphone is left on the stand throughout the "performance," we could move too far from it causing us to be ineffective. If we get too close, it might squawk, whistle, "spit", or announce any other little irritating thing that can cause people to cover their ears to get away from it. These thoughts make us want to take control. We **want** to be in control; however, there are times when we should not be in control.

As with this stationary microphone, if we step away from our Christian life, the message doesn't get out or the message is misunderstood. If we get too close and don't pay attention to the needs of our "audience," we could cause people to back off. We need to find that midpoint. We need to judge our distance appropriately. The easiest way to do this is to make certain that You are always in the center of all of our endeavors. If we ask You to guide us, You will be there, keeping us where we need to be. We need to give up control and leave it to the "professional," the Master technician to find that balance.

To avoid a microphone problem, the media "expert" would probably give us a lapel (or chain) microphone. The specialized microphone is provided by the expert, accepted by us, tested through use, and adjusted according to our individual need—custom fit. This microphone is attached to the person; it becomes a part of that person's apparel. As long as it is allowed to function as it is designed, it will succeed in getting our message across. If we try to take charge of it ourselves, our message could be in jeopardy.

This is reminiscent of our Christian lives. Without Christ, we are like the microphone on the stand. When we take things into our own hands or seek personal control of the situation, we are taking "it" out of the hands of the experts. Once we accept Christ's offer of eternal salvation, we let Him take charge. We, of course, are human and will be tested. We may find that many adjustments become necessary—but, we have eternal access to the master technician.

The process of giving control to Christ is akin to the lapel microphone. To help us in this spiritual process of accepting Christ, we are given the Holy Spirit, indwelled and custom fit according to Your purpose for us. As long as we leave the control up to the Holy Spirit, our Counselor, the message will be heard "loud and clear." If we are meek or weak, we may need to ask for the volume to be turned up. All we need to do is ask.

Father, thank You so much for sending Your Holy Spirit to control our words, actions, and thoughts. Thank You for a world of people to listen to our message. Thank You for our wonderful young people in church. Thank You for the fact that the Holy Spirit asks multiple times throughout the day "Do you hear me now?" Thank You for Your Word so I am able to answer "Loud and Clear." All praise is due Your Holy Name.

I love You.

TO HESITATE OR NOT TO HESITATE

Move in the right direction:
Slow <u>down</u>; speak <u>up</u>; don't be <u>left</u> behind; do what's <u>right</u>.

Yesterday, I was waiting in the car for Bill to come out of a store, and I counted twenty-eight out of fifty cars that did not come to a complete stop at a particular stop sign. (Yes, Father, I do think that, at times, I have too much time on my hands.)

I observed many drivers making "California" stops. In most states, I think they are referred to as "hesitation stops." I thought of the old saying, "He who hesitates is lost."

It seems that at times I get caught up in such a momentum of life that I have a hard time coming to the complete stop as I am instructed. In fact, Father, at the early age of 18, my first and only ticket was for a "California stop." It left a lasting impression (but You know that). The officer was kind and just, but I still received the costly ticket for my violation of the law—another one of my self-inflicted wounds. He was no respecter of persons; he was a respecter of the law, as he should have been.

Sometimes, though, hesitation can be good, Father, for example, when we take the time in our church to stand for the reading of Your Word. This is not a ritual. It doesn't have any soul-saving attributes, but, it is one way I **can** show my respect for the reading of Your Word. In this particular instance a little slowing down, a little hesitation to show respect for the Creator of all things, our heavenly Father, the giver of all things good, is a good thing.

Other good hesitations or even a stop involves taking the time to smile. If I do not take the time when the opportunity presents itself to shake hands or to say "hello," the cost could be a lost prospect of making a new friend, of showing Your love to someone who needs it, or simply of making a visitor feel welcomed. That is, Father, a high price to pay for speeding through life.

Another hesitation which is a good thing is to take the time (which You have given me in the first place) to be sure I am in obedience. When I am in obedience, I receive Your bounty of blessings. If I don't take the time to be obedient, these blessings will be lost, as well as the opportunity to please and glorify You. This is, again, another high price to pay for not taking the time.

If I fail to hesitate long enough to share the Gospel with others or to encourage new Christians in their walk, the burden is so heavy that I don't want to carry it. So, Father, please give me the grace to take a hesitation and a stop in life to be faithful and obedient and loving.

Many other hesitations are not only good, but are necessary for Christians. I must take time to read and think on Your Word. I must take time to pray. I must take time to praise. I need to take time to love and to share. Each one of these carries bountiful blessings.

BUT--the most devastating hesitation of all, Father, is when we hesitate to become Your child. If we hesitate until death takes us, this hesitation brings an eternity of consequence.

Sometimes hesitation is a bad thing, such as in the ticket situation. We should hesitate or stop in our lives to think, but we shouldn't hesitate to do what is right. Every action has its consequence. In my spiritual life, Lord, please grant me the grace to make body-and-soul-saving hesitations and never come to a complete stop until You say "It's time to come home."

I love You.

TAKE YOUR MEDICINE FOR A WALK DAY

You can't sell from an empty shelf.

Today, Father, I had a humorous experience in the doctor's office waiting room. My doctor had asked me to bring all of my medicines to my appointment, so I packed them up in a **b-i-g** box and went to his office. I sat down in the waiting room and looked across the room at a gentleman who had his own large plastic bag full of medicines. He looked at me, in turn, smiled, and said, "This must be *take-your-medicine-for-a-walk-day.*" This statement made me laugh because the collection of medicine was so very large, and it is never out of the house unless I take it with me on a trip, and then I take only what I need. I was taking my medicine for a check-up—what a ridiculous thought.

This consideration caused me to ponder my Christianity: I have a great supply available to me, but, at times, I find I leave it at home until time to take the trip to the church.

In my reflection on the subject, I thought, "Christianity is not to be bottled up or left on a shelf at home." It must be regularly taken out and ingested so the heart can be healed. When a physical heart has been healed, the results are apparent to the onlooker. This is also true of a heart that was spiritually pale, but has been healed—it is noticeable to others and shows through in what I do or say.

If the results of my Christianity are not seen or felt, I need to bring my supply to You for an evaluation and possible refill—I may even need a new prescription for revival.

My mind wandered from the man's statement to "take your dog for a walk." This, I know how to do. It doesn't take much knowledge: If I don't know what to do for part of the way, let my pet lead me—he knows what needs to be done. I do, however, need to have certain supplies with me—necessary for the task at hand.

In general, people look toward their pets for enjoyment or comfort, and the pet is always up for the challenge. For a dog's health and enjoyment, I would take him out for air, exercise, companionship, and socialization. If I keep him housed up, he is comfortable, loved, and happy, but he does not have an opportunity to stretch and to try new things. He learns discipline and teamwork when he goes outside of his comfort zone.

Like this, personally, the more I exercise my Christianity, the stronger it becomes and the more actions I learn to perform with confidence, leading to successful ministry.

Do I take my Christianity, my love for You, out with me daily? Do I take necessary supplies with me for a Christian's walk—my Bible and enlightening or informational tracts? Do I greet others with compassion and warmth? Do I accept them as I, a Christian, should? Or, do I keep my Christianity at home, bottled up, and take it out only on Sundays and Wednesdays? I need, Father, to take my Christianity for a walk throughout the world.

Oh, Father, please grant me Your grace and the blessing of taking my Christianity whenever and wherever I go. Please send Your Holy Spirit to guide my thoughts, actions, and lips so that my life will be "good exercise" for those with whom I come in contact.

I love You.

GREEN, GREEN GRASS OF HOME

". . .; Behold, all things are become new." --II Corinthians 5:17

    The grass is finally coming up for spring, Father, and the wild flowers are starting to bud and are going to be beautiful. It seems as though the fields have been brown and "lifeless" for such a long time—a short time in reality, but it seems like a long, long time. It is the promise of a new season.

    It is wonderful in the valley—home—in the spring and summer while the cattle are still here. Everything is so beautiful and peaceful. The grass is knee-high and Your creatures are so heart-warming and loveable. The colors of the fields are vibrant: the green of the alfalfa and the gold of the grains. The mountains in the far background, the trees in bloom or fruited, and the birds flying all around lift my spirit to new heights.

    Because of our hot, hot summers, most of the large herds of cattle will soon be taken to the cool mountains to feed on the fields of new grass. The farmers, in the cattle's absence, may plant new fields in preparation for their return. In autumn the cattle will, once again, be brought home to the valley area to a promise of plenty before the snow sets in the mountains. Many cattle, unfortunately, will not be found in the hills, and they will perish for lack of food or exposure to extreme cold. How sad.

When the cattle return to the low lands, what a glorious sight. The whole valley will be filled with new life. This is what I call a "God-is-on-His-Throne" day: it is a day for praise and meditation. Only You with Your infinite power and unending love could create something so beautiful and bring it all together, wrapped up in a package of promise for tomorrow: The promise of a new day, the promise of a season, the promise of plenty and joy. (Oh, thank You for the harvests, Father.)

This picture and accompanying feeling led me to think of the words to the song "He Restoreth My Soul." It brought to mind Your promise of everlasting life. We are born into a cold world; it's hard to go through the winters of life. We ask to go "higher with You," but the higher we go, the more we are challenged, and then You, in Your mercy, bring us back into Your valley, again, where we experience Your boundless plenty and goodness, and You restore our souls. You care for us on the mountain, but life is a struggle. But, we still long for Your valley where You give us peace. It doesn't really matter, whether it is in the mountains or in the valley—You keep Your children fed. You protect us wherever Your will leads.

Like the coming home of the cattle, when it's time to come into **Your** valley, some are found and brought into Your Kingdom. Others, unfortunately, are lost because they do not call out for You to save them—and they perish. How tragic. You are faithful and would have saved them, but they have to let You know they want to be saved. Perhaps, nobody—me included—told them how to call out for Your salvation. This isn't only tragic, but it is pitiful negligence.

Your valley, Father, what a wonderful time to look forward to when You take us home: a beautiful valley of an eternity of peace and plenty. We will be fed by Your everlasting love, watered by Your living waters, and welcomed into rest by the majestic songs of the heavenly choir of angels. Again, WOW! I can't imagine how truly beautiful it will be. Thank You for Your mercy and the promise of everlasting life through Christ Jesus.

    I love You.

OUCH! THE YO-YO SYNDROME

Let us hold fast the profession of our faith without wavering (for he is faithful that promised;) --Hebrews 10:23

I'm toying with my weight again. You know, Father, my weight is like a yo-yo: up, down, up, down—all controlled by my action or my lack of action. Loss, gain, loss, double gain—there never seems to be an on/off switch to make it easy. I'm either obedient or disobedient to the laws of good health. Why is that? Oh! Oh! I know why, Father. I am letting my human weakness and harmful desires affect my well-being (more self-inflicted wounds). It seems as though life is a series of opposites: up and down, beginning and end, in and out, right and left, back and forth, right and wrong.

In considering this yo-yo life, I thought about the Christian life. How similar the two situations can be: we have obedient Christians and disobedient Christians. In retrospect, Father, we are all at times disobedient so we have the same on-again, off-again pattern. Why is that? Could it be that we are letting human weakness and harmful desires affect our Spiritual life? Hmmm. If we all sin, then we all have an obedience problem. Some sins may seem larger in our limited view, but we need to realize that **any** sin **is** sin in Your eyes, Father.

Since we sin at times, we need to evaluate our relationship with other Christians who have had a problem. As Christians, we must hold steadfast in our love for our brothers and sisters in Christ. If a brother or sister "messes up," as we all do at times, and is truly sorry and wants to get things right again, we must be there for them. We cannot approve of the **sin**, but we cannot minister to them if we do not still accept **them** as a brother or sister. If a Christian is abandoned because of an error, where will he or she go? I don't even like to guess, Father.

Christians need to see Your love through each other. We need to see Your forgiveness through one another. We need to see our way back to Your path through Your Word and through each other's loving help. We need to have Your Son reflected in our every action. We must be consistent in our Christianity. We need You! We cannot give yo-yo love, Father; by nature and Christ's example there isn't any such thing. Your love is constant, everlasting, and sincere.

A Christian journey generally begins with goals, visions, and plans. Whatever these are should be in accordance with the goals, visions, and plans that You have for each individual. You give us these goals, visions, and plans when hearts are open to You. Your Word assures that if we do not "yo-yo" back and forth, but remain steadfast, we will be fruitful in our ministry. 1 Corinthians 15:58 tells us: *"Therefore, my beloved brethren, be ye steadfast, unmovable, always abounding in the work of the Lord, forasmuch as ye know that your labour is not in vain in the Lord."*

Father, I don't want to be a "yo-yo" Christian: sometimes up, sometimes down, and sometimes just spinning there like a yo-yo. I know, however, that when this does happen, and I ask for You to draw me up, You will snap me back into Your loving, outstretched hands.

I pray to be persistent in my prayer life for my brothers and sisters. I pray that I may be consistent and persistent in my praise and in my study of Your Word. You are worthy of all praise and adoration. You are a great God, a loving God, and an awesome God. You are so gracious, Father. You have given everything a before and after; a beginning and an end. Each morning brings me a new beginning. Please grant me the grace to accept that gift of a new beginning and let my heartstrings be controlled by You.

I love You.

INTO EACH LIFE

"In every thing give thanks: for this is the will of God in Christ Jesus concerning you." --1 Thessalonians 5:18

What a wonderful refreshing rain You gave to us yesterday, Father. Sunshine and rain are such physical and emotional blessings. Humans are so undeniably spoiled and so forgetful. You give the blessing and for "one minute" everybody is happy about it and the next minute it is forgotten and we start complaining. If it is a high temperature; we want rain. If it rains too much, we want the sun.

I see Your attributes when considering the sun, Father: the starting of a new day. The first power I think about is that of Creator: the Creator of all things good. Your power and purpose is perfect. I many times forget this. You cast the light of existence: You gave me the Light in Jesus Christ so I can see beyond my earthly existence--Jesus Christ, the Light of the World. In 1 John 1: 5, You tell me: *". . . and in him is no darkness at all."*

I need to ask for Your light, Father. Without it I stumble through life—unnecessarily and with consequence. Please grant me the grace to always look toward Christ's example and to Your Word for guidance and enlightenment so I don't falter and fail so much. It is a wonderful thing to recall, Father, that no matter how many times I fall, I just need to reach out to You and You will lift me up again to heights only You can give.

Rain? You send rain, Father, and earth receives a beautiful cleansing. The flowers and crops receive much needed water, and the water resources are replenished--but then as human beings (after we think **we've** had enough of it) consider the weather to be dark and gloomy. We seem to overlook the fact that rain **is** needed. It is needed for all nature.

Conversely, too much and too hard of a rain can cause damage to the crops and orchards and can also bring floods.

These are not pleasant, Father, but You are in charge. I will try to give praise in all things because You **are** in charge. I pray, Father, that I may accept with gratitude whatever You send my way—Praise You in all things—in all things give You thanks.

You promise me in 1 Corinthians 10:13 that You will never give me a temptation (or even a storm of life) which cannot be overcome with Your help. *"There hath no temptation taken you but such as is common to man: but God is faithful, who will not suffer you to be tempted above that ye are able; but will with the temptation also make a way to escape, that ye may be able to bear it."*

This is real protection—this is real security from the flood of temptation which comes into my life daily. You tell me in Matthew 28:19-20 that You will be with me always if I am faithful: *"Go ye therefore, and teach all nations, baptizing them in the name of the Father, and of the Son, and of the Holy Ghost: Teaching them to observe all things whatsoever I have commanded you: and lo, I am with you always, even unto the end of the world. Amen."*

All I have to do is be faithful in ministry: in the local church, in the community, in the mission field, and in local, state, and national ministries. I have a choice. I can either go or I can send. I know I can be a part of these ministries through service, giving, and prayer. I can be involved in something larger than life.

Father, You will give me warnings when a "storm in life" may occure because of what I am doing. But You leave it up to me to take caution and avoid the damage. Your Word gives me a step-by-step "how to" in life: it includes the history of human mistakes, the weaknesses of human character, and the solution to all human problems. You provide a storm alert through the Holy Spirit, and a safe haven in my Lord and Savior, Jesus Christ. It is true, into each life some rain must fall; however, while abiding with You, it is a cool, refreshing, and cleansing gift of reassurance of Your love and omnipotence.

I love You.

I SEE YOU

What you see is what you get. Oops!

Father, Aunt Christine and I were on a bus tour last month. (Thank You for my aunt and for journey mercies.) One good thing about taking a bus tour is that we spent our riding time enjoying Your created beauty. It was a trip of multiple pleasures: flowers, trees, desert, history, boats, good food and, of course, window shopping.

You know me, Father; I did take pictures along the way. When I got home and looked at the pictures, I found that there were numerous photos of billboards blocking the beauty that I could have seen. There they were, larger than life. For travelers these billboards may have been a welcomed sight for information. For photographers, they were something to avoid.

How like us, Father, in many ways. Billboards are everywhere. We can't miss them. We, also, are everywhere, telling a message. Every action, word, demeanor is a billboard to those looking. What kind of message are we giving others? Does our message attract or repel? Is it a beneficial or harmful message? Is it a confusing message? Are we so passive that our message is unnoticed? Or, by Your grace, is it a clear, Spirit-filled, welcomed message?

There were two sides to some of the boards. I didn't know what they were showing me unless I looked at the other side. I needed to reposition myself to look at the other side. Other signs were one side only. There wasn't anything "hidden."

Like the billboards, some lives, skills, and talents are used to the maximum, and others are only partially used. The other side is still available for use, waiting for someone to take an interest in developing it with the right message. Do I have another side which needs developing or changing?

A Christian's life can be influential, but we need to be available to those passing us in life. If we do not **make** ourselves available to them, there may never be another opportunity for them to find the help they need and are looking for.

We are all billboards of a sort. We have either attractive or unattractive messages. We can be either helpful or a hindrance to the travelers. We can be either creative or boring. We can be either successful or unsuccessful. We do, however, need to be out there to serve.

At times, Father, it gets discouraging. I feel as though my message isn't getting through at all. But, like the billboard, many times the message gets through but isn't being sought after at the time. Later the message is remembered and looked for. The point is, I can't stop putting Your message out to the public.

Father, I pray I remain consistent in sharing Your message. Please grant me the grace to spread Your Gospel to everyone who comes traveling in my direction.

I love You.

BLOOM WHERE YOU'RE PLANTED

There are no weeds in God's garden.

This is another time for praise and thanksgiving. Oh, thank You, thank You, thank You, Father. We're in Butchart Gardens, once again. As before, it is breathtakingly beautiful. The designer of the gardens divided the garden sections according to type of flower and according to the ability of the particular flower to survive within the environment selected for it.

Not every flower performs the same function: a shrub cannot do the job of a ground cover; a tree cannot take the place of a daisy; a daisy cannot perform the function of a climbing vine; a deep-rooting plant cannot take the place of a hanging plant. Each plant is chosen for a specific purpose and the gardener makes the plan to the benefit of the whole garden.

These particular gardens have bridges, paths, fountains, lawns, performance areas, restaurants, and shopping areas—everything a person might desire while visiting.

You might start on one path, go on it as far as possible, and then change to another path. You are in the same park, but experiencing a different blessing down each path that is taken.

A working church is a lot like this, isn't it, Father? It is full of beauty all around us. When a person first comes into Your family, the surrounding is like that of a beautiful bouquet of flowers: different colors, different sizes, different abilities and/or limitations, different blooming times. I could go on and on, but You know that already, Father.

We spend the first period of our time in the church getting used to what and where things are. We spend time reading the literature (about Your Word and Your church) in order to know our new environment, its mission, its background, and what it is all about.

Once we are settled down and know in which direction we need to go, it's time to head down that path. At times, there are things that block the selected path and we need to choose another route. This is the same as when something causes us to stop serving in the area in which we are currently serving. It is, however, still in the same place and with the same purpose, so it doesn't matter since we're still involved in the "adventure," just starting down a new path.

In a large park, it may be beneficial or necessary to take a plant from a flower bed, and move it to a hanging basket. Or, the plant could be divided, leaving part where it was and the remainder in a new container Likewise, in church, we may be called away from our present mission on to a new mission. This is exciting—a new ministry, new experiences, and new ways of serving. Or, similar to the plant, we may retain our current ministry and just add a second or third one.

There will be a time when we find that we can no longer serve physically. A change is all right, Father. It is a natural course for living things. However, we can always find "something" to do for Your cause. There certainly isn't a lack of things to do. If we drive, we can give someone a ride. We can visit the sick. We can support projects and missionaries. We can send cards. We can serve. Perhaps the most important task of all is that of prayer. We always have something fruitful to give. Praise You, we are always able to pray. The words may not always be readily available, but You promise us in Romans 8:26 that the Spirit will read our hearts and interpret for us. Again, WOW!

There are so many things I can't think of them all; however, I'm certain a leader in the church could help find something which needs a helping hand or two. The main thing is that we don't **wait** for someone to come to us for help if we can find it on our own. We need to find something to do for Your Kingdom.

With flowers, blooms become smaller and smaller when they reach the end of their maturity. Eventually, they are taken up. If they are beautiful, they are brought into the house with others to be enjoyed by their owners. With human beings, tasks become smaller and smaller (not less important) until it is time for You to take us up and bring us into Your home where we can spend an eternity together as planned by You.

    Father, grant me the grace to be gracious and willing to serve. Please grant me the grace to always have something physical or mental that I can contribute to my church. Let me be aware of needs and have what I need to meet those needs.

    I love You.

OLYMPIC "CHAMPIONS"

On God's team there are no heartbreaks or wasted effort.

Terry, Jennifer and I got together for food and fellowship this evening. Of course, we discussed everything friends usually discuss. We laughed a lot, and also discussed the book. The topic finally came around to the 2008 Olympics being held in China. Terry, who was a gymnast in college, shared something with us that I hadn't pondered until now.

She mentioned the rigorous training a gymnast must go through: the spills, bruises, bumps, and tears involved in perfecting just one routine. She mentioned how hard it would be to spend four years getting ready for the Olympics only to have "something" go wrong and watch all Olympic hopes and dreams go down in a matter of seconds with a fall. In some cases, four years of relentless work were tested on a thin board, or dreams were crushed by a slip or a slide on a rain-soaked track. Whatever the cause, they were either eliminated from the competition immediately or reduced in ranking—heartbreak, heartbreak, heartbreak. There isn't much a person can say to make the "pain" go away. Everything they had desired was gone.

What is a "champion," Father? Are there different kinds of champions? champions of heart? champions of strength? champions of endurance? champions of courage? Can a person lose an earthly competition and still be a champion? The dictionary shows the number one definition of "champion" as "valiant fighter." The second definition listed is "person who fights for another or for a cause; defender; protector; supporter." The dictionary further provides "a winner of first place or first prize in a competition" as the third definition of the word.

I'm glad to see that even the dictionary definition of a "champion" does not state that winning is everything. I still like the old saying, "It isn't whether you win or lose, it is how you play the game." Of course, I've never gone through the rigors of training for an athletic event as these wonderful athletes have.

Is being a champion based on skill? If so, all of the athletes are champions. But what if being a champion is based on winning or losing? If so, it is unfortunate that skill is diminished in importance by "winning." Is being a champion based on hard work? If so, again, they are all champions. Is being a champion living and breathing what you are trying to accomplish? If so, they are all champions. My point, Father, is that being a champion should not be based only on whether you win or lose, but should be a matter of fighting the battle physically, mentally, and morally. Of course, then again, we **are** talking strictly about an athletic event.

We have champions, Father: champions of the Faith; champions of eternity. The difference between an earthly **competition** and a heavenly **cause** is: the first is based on human capabilities with one person prevailing, and the other is based on Devine obedience with everyone winning.

Every Christian contributes the gifts that they are given to the cause. We use the abilities we have to pursue the individual tasks given to us for our heavenly cause. As in an athletic competition, the more we "practice" the better we become at it. This includes the child starting by picking up papers around the church to his or her asking friends to ride the bus to church. Senior Saints who are faithful as prayer warriors and serving within their capabilities are serving You with what they have. We all have gifts when we receive the Holy Spirit.

All You ask of us, Father, is that we do our best, that we be obedient, steadfast, and faithful. We are promised that we will end up at the finish line, even though we fall, stumble, or crawl along the way. We may arrive at different times or from different directions, but everyone will cross the finish line. No one following the rules of the cause is left behind. And yes, there are no medals at the end, but a crown is presented by the King. The gold? Revelation 21:21 tells us that the gold is in the streets.

Thank You, Father, for the right to champion any of Your causes You want me to champion. Thank You for making certain that whatever my ability may be, it is adequate enough to cross the finish line with the other "winners." Thank You for giving me training from Your "training manual," Your Word, and from Your coach, my Pastor. And thank You for providing the courage, strength, and patience to finish the course.

You don't tell me that there won't be failures at times. You don't tell me there won't be tears. But even with the tears and failures, I will not have regrets, the feeling of failure, or the feeling that my work was in vain. You are an awesome God.

I love You.

EVERYDAY IS A PAYDAY

Our salvation was not free for Christ

Father, I was thinking about paying bills the other day. (Thank You, Father, that my husband faithfully accepts this responsibility for us.) It seem as though every day has become a payday: one day is payday for us and from then on it's payday for others.

An obligation is incurred as a choice, but carries with it the duty to see it through. There are so many aspects of this responsibility and the paying of the debt. I (We) need to consider so many things.

I need to **reflect**: Did I really need what we're paying for? I need to **verify**: Did I get a product or service for the bill we received? I need to **evaluate**: Is the debt reasonable? I need to **research**: Have I already paid the debt or paid toward its resolution? I need to **question**: Have I overpaid? Have I underpaid and fallen short of reasonable expectations? I need to **persevere**: Will I ever be able to pay it all? I may have cause for and need to **be thankful**: Has the debt been forgiven?

I can't think of the word "debt," Father, without thinking of the largest debt of all: the debt I owe to Christ for His sacrifice. In thinking of my list of questions above, I thought of them relative to my spiritual debt. I owe this debt daily, however, the benefits last an eternity.

I do need to **reflect**: Did I really need what I'm paying for? Every time I reflect on my salvation, I know beyond a shadow of doubt that I did, absolutely, need salvation.

I have **verified** that I have received the product or service for the debt I owe. I have been assured that I **have** received salvation and eternity with You through Your Word. *"These things have I written unto you that believe on the name of the Son of God; that ye may **know** that ye have eternal life, and that ye may believe on the name of the Son of God."* --1 John 5:13 (emphasis mine). This is a promise, a personal message of assurance to me. I'm not told that I "might" have eternal life or that if I work hard enough, or If I'm a good person I'll have eternal life, but, instead, I am told that if I believe on the name of the Son of God I may KNOW I have eternal life.

I have **evaluated** the reasonableness of the debt. Father, it's like the old song says, "Jesus paid it all. All to Him I owe." He gave His life for me so anything asked of me in Your Word is reasonable recompense.

I have **researched.** Have I already paid the debt or paid toward its resolution? According to Your Word and considering my human disobedience, I haven't paid back much at all, but I'm making an honest effort.

I have **questioned**: Have I overpaid? As we hear so much in today's conversations, Father, "in no way" have I overpaid. Have I underpaid and fallen short of reasonable expectations? Oh, yes, Father. How could I, in this world, ever repay what I owe? I can't.

I will, with Your strength, **persevere**: I will never be able to pay my debt in full, but I can pay on my account with my love, my obedience, and my honor. I can communicate regularly with You and read what You have given me to read.

There is no fine print in this contract: everything is written with my understanding and my benefit in mind—it speaks to me loudly and clearly.

I do have cause for and need to **be thankful**: Has the debt been forgiven? Yes. Jesus paid it all for me. It was a gift. *"For by grace are ye saved through faith; and that not of yourselves: it is the gift of God: Not of works, lest any man should boast."* --Ephesians 2:8-9

Every day I go deeper in debt in the form of blessings, answered prayer, and every good thing received. These are all worthy debts. The only way I can pay back is by being a blessing to others, by giving You praise, and to give only my best to You in praise and in obedience.

I can boast of two things only, Father. I can boast of heaven as my home for eternity and I can boast that I am justified to enter into Your presence. I will know that my sin debt has been forgiven—paid in full.

My appreciation, praise, thanksgiving, obedience, and love I give to You in partial payment for giving me Your Son as a sacrifice for the remission of my sin. I rejoice in declaring every day as payday on my debt to Christ.

I love You.

BROKEN FENCES

God specializes in fixing broken people

We had to repair our back fence last month, Father. It was unsightly and broken in some areas and beyond use. The boards had holes all the way through where they were not shielded against the weather. The wood was fractured and peeled away. It was a sad, sad mess. It needed renewal—a new lease on "life." The fence couldn't fix itself, so Bill and his brother from Colorado determined to fix the "ills" of the fence. They went to the store and purchased what was needed for repair of the fence.

A broken fence is very similar to a life, isn't it, Father: a fence can be broken and a life can be broken. A life can become unsightly and "full of holes." If a fence is broken, it stops doing the job for which it was created. Similarly, lives, when they are broken, are unable to perform their purpose in life which has been given by You: things which should be kept inside creep out, and things which should be kept out, invade the inside where it isn't welcome.

In such cases, as with the fence needing repair and a life needing revival, help is essential. Neither the fence nor a life can mend itself or hide from the observer that it is, indeed, in need of some tender loving care.

We need Your "tender loving care" to repair or replace the broken parts, refinish Your covering—which has been abused—and patch up the holes "life" has left. We need You, Your shepherds, and our brothers and sisters in Christ to complete the renewal and repair. The only tools necessary are love, compassion, Your Word, and prayer. These are all provided by You and through Christ's example.

The condition of our fence affects more than one family. It affects the neighbors to the right, left, and beyond the fence in back. We have new neighbors on the right (they are great neighbors, thank You, Father) so they haven't been there long enough to notice the deterioration of the boards. Otherwise, they would probably have offered to share in the labor and in the expense of repairing the barrier.

Similar to the condition of our fence affecting more than one family, a broken life affects everyone with whom it comes in contact. It affects our family, our friends, strangers—and our ministry. Who can help? Everyone can help with Your guidance. The new brothers and sisters have not been with us long enough to have noticed the deterioration of our lives. Otherwise, they would probably offer to share in the labor of repairing the barrier. They, can, however, assist when told what needs to be done next. (Thank You, Father, for Your loving family of believers.)

Father, when I notice a brother, sister, or stranger displaying holes in their lives, please grant me Your grace to take up my tools of love, compassion, Scripture, and prayer and get to work to help patch things up and put pieces together again. Let me offer to share in the labor, and in the pains which comes along with the labor, so that the job can be completed and the life can be made whole again to Your glory.

When a job for You has been completed, I will glory in its beauty.

I love You.

AN AMAZING BLANKET OF WHITE

As gentle as falling snow, Your spirit covers me.

This is, again, a time of praise and thanksgiving to You, Father—my Creator, my Savior, and my Comforter—all wrapped up in One. You are an awesome God.

Do You know how amazingly beautiful Your blanket of snow is to me, Father? (Oh, of course You do. Forgive me for my lapse of memory while we are visiting in my thoughts.) The beauty of the snow is one of the "side effects" You have planned for me and all of Your children in Your creation. Beauty! Beauty! Beauty! As I looked at some pictures of a trip through the California mountains, I was inspired in my memories.

I was inspired by the way one flake flows into another and into another, creating a beautiful covering of snow: each flake totally different, yet somehow, fitting and merging. I was thinking of how I am revived by the cool air. I am refreshed by the clean smell of the air as it is cleansed by the white flakes descending to the earth to cover everything exposed to it—adding to everything's individual splendor.

As with everything on earth, Father, some things exposed to the elements for too long of a time cannot be covered up. But if it is made available to Your blessing coming down, it will be cleaned up. You plan everything item by item. Much like Your planning of Christ's sacrifice on the cross to cover all of my sins. Every once in a while it is necessary to reach down and remove handfuls of "dirty snow" to keep my life as You want it to be and the way I want the casual observer to see You.

Oh, thank You, Father, for blessings upon blessings which You send down showering my life with a blanket of beauty, love, and hope. This is one time I can feel "flakey" and it is okay. I don't want to shake it off or brush it off. It is a covering for eternity. Thank You for the covering of the purity of Christ and for His example. Thank You for the plan of Salvation

You so perfectly and simply set down for me in Your Word,. Thank You for my family and my church family, and thank You, Father, for Pastor and his family.
    I love You.

THE GOOD NEWS

Father, this book has been a fun (and revealing) time of putting down my thoughts; however, some things should not be left to the imagination. Your Good News is one of those things: It is real. It is unimaginable. It is joy. It is life fulfilled. Acts 17:30 tells me, in part: *"...but now commandeth all men everywhere to repent."* This is not a suggestion. It is a commandment so I feel I **_must_** end this series of love letters to You by thanking You for Your plan of salvation. I feel I would be remiss if I did not share that story with others.

The steps You give us are so simple to follow, but are too important to take lightly. It is the most important decision a human being can make. You left the decision up to each individual once the facts are known.

First, realize that You love each individual person: John 3:16: ***"For God so loved the world that he gave his only begotten Son that whosoever believeth in him should not perish but have everlasting life."***

Second, we need to realize that sin causes **_all_** to fall short. Romans 3:23: ***"For all have sinned and come short of the glory of God."***

Third, we need to realize that sin has a price that must be paid. Romans 6:23: ***"For the wages of sin is death but the gift of God is eternal life, through Jesus Christ our Lord."***

Fourth, We need to accept the fact that Christ died to pay that price. Romans 5:8 : ***"But God commendeth his love toward us in that while we were yet sinners, Christ died for us."***

Finally, we must **_pray_**, **_confess_** and **_repent_** of our sins, and ask Jesus to be our Saviour, and claim Your promise of eternal life. Romans 10:13: ***"For whosoever shall call upon the name of the Lord shall be saved."***

Five simple steps, Father. It doesn't seem many when compared with all of the steps Christ took up Mount Calvary.

What does this mean? For certain, it means that we have eternal security when we give our life over to Christ. We are assured of this in one of Your promises. 1 John 5:13

"These things have I written unto you that believe on the name of the Son of God; that ye may know that ye have eternal life, and that ye may believe on the name of the Son of God."

This is all it takes to become free, isn't it, Father? Believe on the name of Jesus Christ and a few other simple steps for us, which came at a very complicated and high price for Christ. Thank You, Father for giving us Your Son to secure our freedom from sin and eternity with You in heaven. This is truly freedom.

I love You.

FREEDOM ISN'T FREE

I had one final "revelation," Father. I watched the news this week. I feel negligent that I don't watch the news regularly because it does affect me, but, it is so negative and depressing. Nothing is as it used to be. I'm sure the younger generation gets tired of hearing this, but then, they don't have the advantage of seeing how wonderful America used to be. I don't mean it isn't still the most wonderful country in the world. What I do mean is that it is different from years past. I could spend pages talking about the differences I've seen from 40, 50, 60 years ago, but that is unnecessary for our visit now.

What all of this is coming to, Father, is that I think the difference is in attitude toward, and interpretation of, "rights." It seems as though the contemporary definition of rights is that a person has the right to do anything he or she chooses to do as long as he or she doesn't break the law—or get caught.

When I was growing up, a person had the right to do anything he or she wanted to do—as long as it didn't interfere with someone else's rights. Then, the rights needed to be modified for all persons involved. The essence of what I am considering is that in past decades we acknowledged that rights and freedom are not free. They carry with them the inherent element of assumed responsibility for actions and the acceptance of consequences if we choose to not fulfill our responsibility.

Father, I want to talk with You about a spiritual freedom that concerns me (Thank You, Father, for giving us free will): the subject I am concerned with is that of spiritual growth. In the larger scheme of things it is a conscious and team effort to learn and grow as a Christian. This is not meant to be judgmental discussion, Father, but strictly observational.

We have discussed previously about getting the whole story in church. Many times, the pastor of the church does his best to give the whole story, but people are not where they should be to hear it. It is like the old saying, he's "preaching to the choir."

There are so many of us who are simply not growing. At times most of us do suffer a period lacking in growth. I am sure we are sincere about our salvation and we are secure in the fact that we will spend eternity in heaven; however, we, at times, forget about the responsibility that comes with our salvation.

Salvation, unlike freedom, *is* free, paid for in full by Your Grace through the sacrifice of Christ. Salvation is so simple for us to receive that I feel we occasionally become lazy and rest in our salvation, forgetting about our Christian responsibility. Some of us stop right after receiving the greatest gift of all, our salvation through Christ. This gift, if we are in obedience to scripture, includes the wonderful things of life which fill the heart to tearful gratitude. If we stop our Christian growth at the point of salvation, it's like accepting a gift, opening the package, thanking the person, but not taking the lid off of the box to receive what is inside. Why does this sometimes happen?

It is possibly because we are told what we are expected to do to gain salvation. We follow through with accepting Christ as our savior; we go through the waters of baptism and then, so many of us rest at that point because—we don't know what to do after that. Others may "fall through the cracks" because of someone's—*my*—lack of follow through. Church soon becomes a place we go to only on special occasions or when there isn't something "more pressing" to do.

We seem to call on You whenever we are in need of something, but, somehow, praise and thanksgiving are left out. We, it seems, read anything before we read the Bible. We read inspirational books; we read "self-help" books (which aren't all bad); we read people's interpretation of the Bible; but worst of all, Father, is we, at times, read people instead of reading Your Word. We then justify our actions or lack of actions based on these other people who profess to be Christians. The new Christian under these circumstances ends up looking in the wrong place for an example to follow. He or she isn't experienced enough in Your Word to know that.

Whose responsibility is that, Father? Is it a result of free will or is it a matter of lack of follow through? If it's free will, well, You gave that to us. But, Father, if it is for lack of follow through by Your saints, shame on us.

My prayer, now, Father, is that we (*I*) who have had the advantage of being discipled by pastors, parents, teachers, or Christian friends remain faithful in the reading of Your Word and in prayer. I pray that we are fervent in our Faith and hold out our hands and our hearts to disciple new Christians while they are anxious to learn and are excited in their new salvation. I pray that we show them by Your Word and a Godly example, affording them the opportunity to grow in knowledge and obedience and awe: awe of Your omnipotence, of Your omnipresence, of Your plan for eternity, and of Your never-ending wonders and joy.

We are told multiple times in Your Word about walking Your walk, Father—to walk in the Spirit. If we don't read Your Word and don't know what Your path is, how can we do that?

I was pondering ways to grow in knowledge which could be passed on to new brothers or sisters in Christ. The most available and obvious to me are:

1. Read Your Word daily: the authorized King James Version without "unauthorized" changes for convenience sake.

2. Pray and search for the working of the Holy Spirit. Those who have accepted Christ as their Savior have the Holy Spirit now. Call on Him.

3. Find a Bible-preaching church and meet the pastor. We need to be in church **regularly** to be fed and to receive our spiritual nutrition for growth. If we miss church, we risk becoming "anemic" in many important areas of our lives: love, control, hospitality, charity, peace, and other attributes of Your Spirit. We have access to these qualities the minute we

become Your child and if we don't know how to call upon the Spirit, we need to be taught and we need to learn and do.

4. Find "busy-in-the-Lord's-work" friends from whom we can learn. We need to have these new friends teach us from Your Words **only**. Not man's words, but Your words. Study books are good if they are grounded in Your Word.

5. Pray without ceasing with praise and thanksgiving included. You, Father, Christ, and the Holy Spirit are worthy of all praise and all glory, and all is due Your names.

6. Avoid places, things, and activities that are contrary to our own—or someone else's—spiritual growth. The places may not in and of themselves be bad, but they may not be beneficial for spiritual growth. We must accept that one of our Christian responsibilities is not to lead someone else "astray." We are to be examples, and as such, we must be good and Godly examples. We need to call upon Your Spirit daily to take control of our lives for the day. Some days I need to call upon Your Spirit multiple times a day for help. Someone is "learning" from us, and we need Your guidance. The Spirit, praise You, Father, **is** always with us for the asking.

7. Share Christian joy and knowledge with others. Offer them the saving knowledge of Christ and go the step beyond by teaching them. Help them enjoy the whole of what You have for us.

These are all positive steps, Father. If we honestly admit that we do not do one of these steps, give us the grace to ask for guidance.

My personal prayer, Father, is that Your Spirit continues to convict or chastise me when I step off of Your path so that I can be considered a worthy child to be called Christian—with human failings as all humans, but yielding my soul and my heart to Your will.

All of these steps, Father, come after salvation, don't they? This is where my responsibility begins. Thank you. You are an awesome Father to all of Your children. Although I grieve You from time-to-time, You are faithful to Your promises and Your mercy is everlasting. Thank You for Your forgiveness,

Father, giving peace through obedience, knowledge through study, and persistence through faith.
  I love You.

(I invite you, if you have received Christ as Savior or if something in these "love letters" has been a particular blessing to you, to please e-mail a note to us and share the blessing. (jchapman15@comcast.net)

AND THE GRACE OF OUR LORD JESUS CHRIST BE WITH YOU ALL. AMEN.

--PHILIPPIANS 4:23